Dissident Syria

MAKING OPPOSITIONAL ARTS OFFICIAL

By miriam cooke

Paperback   Price: $21.95
             ISBN: 978-0-8223-4035-5

Library cloth Price: $74.95
             ISBN: 978-0-8223-4016-4

Pages: 184 pages (estimate)
13 black and white illustrations

Publication date: August 2007

COVER DESIGN NOT FINAL

For additional information contact:

Laura Sell
Publicity
Ph: 919-687-3639
Fax: 919-688-4391
lsell@dukepress.edu
www.dukeupress.edu

Duke University Press
905 West Main St.
Suite 18B
Durham, NC 27701

Dissident Syria

Duke University Press Durham & London 2007

© 2007 Duke University Press
All rights reserved
rinted in the United States of America on
acid-free paper ⊛
Designed by C. H. Westmoreland
Typeset by Tseng Information Systems, Inc.
Library of Congress Cataloging-in-
Publication data appear
on the last printed page of this book.

Acknowledgments

INTRODUCTION

contents

acknowledgments

There are many I would like to thank for their help in this project.

Thanks to the Fulbright Scholarship program for funding my initial research during six months in Syria between 1995 and 1996.

While there I benefited immeasurably from my conversations with Hasan Abbas, Mamduh ʿAdwan, Mustafa ʿAli, Sadiq al-ʿAzm, Hala al-Faisal, Alberto Fernandez, Nadia al-Ghazzi, Ulfat Idilbi, Ghassan al-Jabaʿi, Muhammad Malas, and Marjorie Ransom.

For willingness to participate in the colloquium that changed the course of my research, thank you to Colette al-Khuri, Huda Naamani, Nadia Khust, and Mallahat al-Khani.

Thanks to the Rockefeller Institute and to Muhsin al-Musawi, Muhammad Shahin, Jale Parla, and Hager Ben Driss for ten amazing days in Bellagio, where we wrestled with the many and conflicting meanings of dissidence and creativity.

I am fortunate to have been given several occasions to try out parts of this book in different venues. I would like to thank Bill Granara at Harvard University for the first opportunity in the United States to present my thoughts about my meetings with Syrian intellectuals; Elisabeth Boyi and Bob and Mary Layne Gregg at Stanford University and Elizabeth Thompson and Farzaneh Milani at the University of Virginia at Charlottesville for inviting me to to discuss Syrian film; Monika Kaup at the University of Washington in Seattle for providing a forum in which to mull over similarities between Asad's Syrian state and W's U.S. regime.

Thanks to Susan Slyomovics and MR and LM (who know who they are) for many enlightening conversations about prisons and other ways of thinking about dissent.

Warmest thanks to friends and colleagues who have helped me over the past ten years to make sense of my Syrian experiences: Eula and Paul Hoff, Guo-Juin Hong, John Kador, Satti Khanna, Claudia Koonz, Ebrahim Moosa, Negar Mottahedeh, and Bernie Avishai.

But as always it is to Bruce that I owe my greatest debt of gratitude. Always inspiring, always attentive, always enthusiastic, he is my best critic, my dearest friend.

Dissident Syria

A single sparrow
Its chirp without echo
A space between rocks and houses
Where poppies dwell in seclusion
Image of a horse on my wall
And the wind lashes the trees
And I, waiting for the knock on the door
Sleep is destined for
Those who were not created for it:
The wind
River water
The fish
And my heart
Endless possibilities
Like the first drops of rain
On dust
Like the opening of the poppies
As far as the eye can see
—MAMDUH 'ADWAN, "Minorities"

introduction

A month after the invasion of Iraq in March 2003 the Bush administration declared Iraq's neighbor Syria to be a "rogue state." Since that time Syria has been linked with Iraq as a sponsor of international terrorism and a military dictatorship. It is both. At least, the state is. Yet there is another Syria: a country where dissident patriots seek a space to express their conscience and their creativity in circumstances unimaginable to most outsiders. In *Dissident Syria: Making Oppositional Arts Official*, I traverse the abyss between these two Syrias, between the power of the state and the power of culture. It is this other Syria, largely unknown to Americans, that I want to bring to light in the pages that follow.

Between autumn 1995 and spring 1996, I lived in Syria. I had come to learn about the literary scene, and I was particularly interested in women writers. Although Syrian writers in exile are well known, those who have remained inside are little known abroad. Soon after arriving in Damascus I met with some women writers. Colette al-Khuri and Ulfat Idilbi were pioneers of feminist literature in the region and, along with writers like Nadia al-Ghazzi, Nadia Khust, and Mallahat al-Khani, they were active members of the literary establishment. In October I organized and chaired a symposium on their works (chapters 2 and 3).

Then one evening at the home of the playwright Mamduh 'Adwan (1941–2004), I was asked why I was spending so much time with the women and was not looking at film, theater, and the writings of men. Didn't I want to understand what was really going on in Syria? Of course I did, I protested, I had already learned a great deal. The conversation drifted back to Mamduh's new play, *The Ghoul* (chapter 5). Shortly before the evening ended, the filmmaker Muhammad Malas (b. 1945) took me aside and told me point-blank that I should read prison literature by people like Ibrahim Samuil and Ghassan al-Jaba'i.

"Prison narratives reflect our daily life." 'Adwan had joined us.

"A talented writer brings the reader into an unfamiliar, imagined space," Malas said. "He makes it so real that it seems to be inhabited, familiar. The time Ghassan and Ibrahim spent in prison has given them a special vision, a unique style. The importance of *adab al-sujun* [prison literature] is that it exists. Its mere presence on the stage of literature shows that it is relevant to the average reader and that it is not exceptional. Ghassan is writing about an experience we share. It is so familiar. We don't have to go to prison to appreciate their stories. Ghassan represents the best in modern literature. He takes us back to the sadness of Chekhov."[1]

The prison of daily life overshadowed much of the culture I studied. Intellectuals were looking for ways to resist the stifling climate that prevailed during the last years of Hafiz Asad's thirty-year rule, and they faced a dilemma: the state that controlled and sometimes silenced them also needed them.

When the Berlin wall fell, the long-time autocrat became even more intolerant of dissent. Socialism had collapsed in Eastern Europe and the capitalists had waged their victorious 1991 Gulf War. The Arab world split into opposing camps, and Syria was forced into a contradictory political position. It retained its hard-liner stance vis-à-vis Israel and the United States even while flirting with "Western" notions of capitalism and democracy. To manage such paradoxical policies, the state used culture to shape public opinion and to legitimate its power. To grasp some of the complexities of this relationship between the regime and its intellectuals, we need to cast a glance back into history.

In 1947 Syria gained its independence from French mandatory rule. During the following fifteen years, leaders rose and fell at an alarming rate. Behind the scenes in 1959 a small group of military officers posted to Cairo formed the secret "Military Committee." They were committed to Baathism, a pan-Arab ideology behind a party that came into being in the 1940s. The Baathists were secular socialists who extolled the Arab nation, regardless of ethnicity, religion, and language, and called for its *baath*, or revival. By insisting on the primacy of the Arab nation, the Baathists could claim that Islam had flowered as a cultural expression of Arabism, not as a universal religion. Baathism was attractive to the heterodox Alawites, Syria's largest religious minority. Most members of the Military Committee were Alawites, including Hafiz Asad (1930–2000), a young man from the village of Qardaha in the Ansariya Mountains of northern Syria.

The Alawites were linked to the Nusayri religious sect, an offshoot of Shiite Islam. Formed in the middle of the ninth century, it is "the only branch of extreme Kufan Shiism which has survived into the contemporary period." Nusayris professed both metempsychosis and antinomianism, leading to a fourteenth-century fatwa that condemned the Nusayris "as more heretical even than idolators" (*Encyclopedia of Islam* [Leiden: Brill]). It was Ibn Taymiyya[2] who authorized a jihad against the Nusayris because they venerated 'Ali b. Abi Talib (the cousin and son-in-law of the Prophet Muhammad and his fourth successor) above Muhammad. The name Alawite derives from 'Ali. By the nineteenth century, the Syrian Alawites had become "an oppressed and exploited minority who often worked as sharecroppers.

. . . As part of their 'divide and rule' tactics, French Mandate officials recruited large numbers of 'Alawis into their army, thereby exacerbating tensions between rural 'Alawis and urban Sunnis" (Salamandra 2004, 9).

These tensions came to a head in March 1963, when young Baathists deposed President Nazim al-Qudsi. Forming the National Command, they established Baath Party rule in the country and declared martial law. More than forty years later, this state of emergency persists, with the pretext that Syria is at war with Israel. Government ministers were given extraordinary powers: the prime minister became the martial law governor, with the minister of interior as his deputy. Baath officials have the license to "arrest preventively anyone suspected of endangering public security and order, and to authorize investigation of persons and places at all times, and to delegate any person to perform these tasks" (Human Rights Watch/Middle East [HRW/ME], July 1995, 3). On 23 February 1966, the Military Committee seized those positions they had not yet taken: Hafiz Asad was appointed minister of defense and Salah Jadid become Syria's leader. For the first time in Syrian history Alawites held the two most powerful positions in a country that Damascene Sunni Muslims had traditionally ruled.

It is the relationship with Israel that defines Baathist Syria. In 1967, the Israelis captured the Golan Heights and sacked its main city, Kuneitra. Some criticized the regime, especially the minister of defense, for its handling of the war.[3] The 1967 War was mourned as a calamity throughout the Arab world, and in Syria it reaffirmed the need for martial law. Until today the Golan is occupied and it remains a bone of contention in all of the failed negotiations between Syria and Israel.

Linked to Israel is the question of Palestine. It hung heavy over Syrian politics because support of Palestine was integral to Baathist ideology. The 1967 War increased pressure on Palestinians everywhere, but especially in Jordan, where the recently legitimized Palestine Liberation Organization (PLO) had established its military and political headquarters. By 1970 Jordan's King Husayn determined to oust the PLO leadership, and in September, later called Black September, he achieved his goal. Hafiz Asad had ordered tanks to the Jordanian border to help the Palestinians, but when the Jordanian air force started to bombard them he withdrew. In the aftermath, some Palestinians moved to Syria while the leadership established its new headquarters in Beirut.

The 1967 War and Black September undermined Salah Jadid's credibility, and Hafiz Asad attacked his former ally. He deposed Jadid and incarcerated him in the Mezze prison on the hill. From November 1970 until his death in 1993, Jadid remained in prison. Nevertheless, he retained his supporters, who are called Shubatis, or February partisans (the Arabic *shubat* means February) in memory of the 23 February 1966 coup that brought him to power. In conversation, the prison writer Ghassan al-Jaba'i (b. 1945) called Jadid a real gentleman, "a modest man for whom a Volkswagen was sufficient luxury" (see also Seale 1989, 105, 107–109). Until the early 1980s, the Shubatis enjoyed a degree of freedom, but then the government cracked down on all opposition groups (chapter 7).

Immediately upon seizing power, Hafiz Asad launched his *haraka tashihiya*, or Corrective Movement, so called to avoid the impression that there had been dissension at the top and that his military actions could be called a coup. During the early years, Asad tried to ingratiate formerly alienated Baathists and to attract new supporters. The political climate became more liberal as the new ruler attempted to forge national unity and loyalty. He even tolerated the publication and staging of works critical of the regime (Seale 1989, 170–173).

The 1973 October War against Israel, however ambiguous the outcome, gave Asad an extra boost. It was on 6 October 1973 (the Jewish Day of Atonement, or Yom Kippur) that Asad and Egyptian president Anwar Sadat launched a surprise attack on Israel from north and south. After initial successes, the Syrians and the Egyptians were driven back; on 22 October, bruised by the vehemence of the Israeli retaliation, they agreed to a ceasefire. Both sides claimed that their mission had been successfully accomplished. For the Syrians and the Egyptians, the early "victories were trumpeted by the official Arab media and the later setbacks glossed as if they did not matter" (Seale 1989, 234). Claiming it to be a magnificent victory, Asad attached the name Tishrin, or October, to the war and emblazoned the name on buildings, monuments, a university, and a newspaper.

Yet the propagandistic front overlaid a tightening infrastructure. Asad oversaw a Soviet-style single-party police state, with "a network of fifteen competing intelligence agencies that spied on his own people" (MacFarquhar 2000). Article 8 of the constitution established the Baath Party as the leader of both society and the state.

Asad drew on precedents for his praetorian practices. He strengthened censorship laws that had been introduced in the mid-nineteenth century and that were sporadically reinforced during the twentieth century. First the Ottomans and then the French in the 1920s had instituted strict laws about what could and could not be published. They regulated writings, cultural societies, and printing presses to such an extent that many intellectuals fled to Egypt or Europe (Farah 1977, 164–167, 179–180). The French also "shut down newspapers, theaters, and cinemas, tightly controlled the only radio station, and imposed their authority over schools and universities" (HRW 1991, 110). They even intervened in the making of films.[4] The influence of French forms of censorship and control over the distribution of cultural production persists today in government agencies like the National Film Organization (chapter 6).

During the twenty-three years following independence in 1947, a succession of coups kept intellectuals in a state of constant alert. Martial law imposed since 1963 and strengthened in 1970 had given the state absolute control over the production of culture and the distribution of information. Article 4 of the State of Emergency Law specified that the purview of the censor included "letters and communications of all kinds. Censorship of newspapers, periodicals, drawings, printed matter, broadcasts and all means of communication, propaganda and publicity before issue; also their seizure, confiscation and suspension" (*Index on Censorship* 1984, vol. 13, no. 2, 36). Press employees holding key positions had to be Baath members. All newspapers had to be officially authorized, and few were (HRW/ME 1995, 10). In 1969, Asad acknowledged the symbolic importance of the press by sending "his tanks into Damascus, straight to the offices of *Al-Ba'th* and *Al-Thawra* [newspapers] as well as to the Damascus broadcasting station. He removed their top editors and installed his loyalists" (HRW 1991, 113). To control the press was to control the country.

Taboo subjects included "politics, ideology, religion, society, and economics, and especially discussions of Syria or the Middle East. . . . The censors ban any book that refers to Alawites or to sectarian differences, excluding for this reason virtually all Western studies of contemporary Syria" (HRW 1991, 123, 127). Whoever did not acknowledge the greatness of the leader, in other words, did not participate in what political scientist Lisa Wedeen (1999) has called the "Asad cult," was accused of crimes against the state.[5]

Manuscripts and screen scripts had to be submitted to censorship committees attached to the Ministry of Culture or Information, which stamped each approved page. The Ministry of Information "keeps a list of censored books; and it makes spot checks on all bookshops to ensure that no banned book is on sale or even in stock." Songs, scientific programs, lectures by foreign scholars, and even Friday sermons in the mosques had to be approved (Sadiq 1990).

Censorship of the press extended to Lebanon after 1976, when the Syrian military intervened in the civil war on behalf of Maronite Christians. Nowhere else in the Arab world would press censorship have had the same impact, for Beirut had long been a haven of free speech. The Syrians closed down publishing houses whose editorial policies they did not like and they punished recalcitrant editors. The case of Salim al-Lawzi, editor of *Al-Hawadith*, is especially poignant. In 1980, Lawzi tried to escape Syrian censorship by leaving Beirut for London. When his mother died he decided to risk the trip to Lebanon to attend her funeral, but upon his return he was killed (HRW 1991, 121). Lest there be any ambiguity about the reason for his assassination, his writing hand was burned with acid. The message was clear: no Syrian or Lebanese journalist could evade the long arm of the Syrian state.

Hafiz Asad was a leader quite unlike his predecessor. Whereas Salah Jadid had refused to call himself head of state, understanding the problem inherent in an Alawite claiming the right to "a post traditionally reserved for Sunnis" (Seale 1989, 105), Asad boldly staked his claim. He fashioned a Sunni Muslim facade to cover his Alawite identity. He based his strategy on a syllogistic argument that went something like this: the 1973 constitution stipulated that Islam was the religion of the state; Asad was head of a state whose leader had to be a Muslim; ergo President Hafiz Asad was a Muslim. But was he really? Some have argued that the heterodox Alawites could never be considered Muslims. Many Sunnis, not accepting the ascription of divinity to humans, consider the Alawite reverence for a quasi-divine 'Ali to be blasphemous. They also distrust the secrecy surrounding the rituals and tenets of the Alawites. Consequently, not only Ibn Taymiyya but many of his successors reject outright the Alawite claim to be Muslims.

Nonetheless, Asad had himself declared the head of a state whose leader had to be a Muslim. To achieve this coup he enlisted the help of Imam Musa al-Sadr, head of the Higher Shiite Council in Lebanon. In July 1973, Sadr issued a fatwa proclaiming the Alawites to be "an authentic part of Shi'i Islam" (Seale 1989, 352; see also 173). Mysteriously in 1978 the imam disappeared, but Hafiz Asad made good his claim by praying in public. In 1987, on the seventeenth anniversary of the Corrective Movement, Asad publicly professed his belief "in God and the message of Islam. . . . I was, I am and I will remain a Muslim, just as Syria will remain a proud citadel flying high the flag of Islam! But the enemies of Islam who traffic in religion will be swept away!" (quoted in Seale 1989, 328; see also Van Dam 1996, 142–143). Intellectuals were not fooled, and some mocked the autocrat's religious theatrics (chapter 5).

Asad focused on architecture to establish his Islamic credentials. He built numerous mosques all over the country, including a massive mosque in memory of his mother in his native village of Qardaha.[6] After his eldest son and heir apparent, Basil, died in a car accident in 1994, Asad erected what amounts to a Muslim saint's shrine complex. Basil did not die fighting for a cause, but he was still called a *shahid,* or martyr, someone close to a saint. When visiting Qardaha in the summer of 1994 I went to the shrine. From afar I could hear the monotonous chanting of the Qur'an: throughout the seven months since Basil's death, the Qur'an had been recited uninterruptedly for

The shrine of Basil Asad in 1994 in Qardaha,
with photograph of Basil on the hajj.

twenty-four hours a day. The tomb was draped in the green cloth
reserved for Muslim saints. It was surrounded with military memo-
rabilia. On the left was a photograph of Basil wearing the *ihram*, or
pilgrim's seamless white cloth. Before dying, Basil had performed
the Muslims' most sacred ritual of the hajj to Mecca.

The shrine was part of a complex filled with images of Basil and
his father. One in particular links the young martyr to Muhammad,
the Prophet of Islam. Mounted on a horse flying wingless to the heavens, a haloed Basil in military uniform turns to wave one last time to
his father, who stands below, hands held out in ritual prayer. In the
distance is a crowd of tiny worshippers, each in the same ritual pose,

as though lined up behind the mosque imam. This scene of a flying horse soaring through the skies is a clear citation of the Prophet Muhammad's famous *mi'raj*, or night journey. Mounted on Buraq, a kind of Muslim Pegasus, the Prophet one night was taken from Jerusalem up through the seven heavens until he found himself in the presence of the Almighty. It is on this occasion that the five daily prayers were prescribed for Muslims. The message is clear: in this representation of his son's ascension, Hafiz Asad becomes father to one whose saintliness rivals that of the Prophet.

Still another example of Hafiz Asad's mobilization of architecture to bolster his religious credentials can be seen in the famous Umayyad Mosque in the old city of Damascus.[7] Asad had it restored in the 1980s and 1990s, but with a difference: he had his own name inscribed on the top of one of the minarets as patron of the renovation. Although the inscription can be seen only through a camera's zoom lens,[8] its power reverberates in the Syrian public square. This kind of performative writing, to use John Bodel's term, can be traced back to the Romans. Bodel writes that in some religious contexts, inscriptions were not supposed to be read "but to represent through their writing that particular acts had been duly performed" (2001, 19–20). In some cases, these inscriptions were so carved and so placed that they would be barely legible. What mattered was that the act of inscribing had been piously performed and was widely acknowledged.

In Asad's case, the minaret was inscribed in such a way that it also would look like a pious act, for God's eyes alone. After all, it was only God who could see it unaided by plane or zoom lens. But then, it was photographed and prominently displayed on a UNESCO brochure.[9]

Having established the Muslim veneer Asad could take on those who challenged his religious credentials, specifically the Sunni Muslim Brothers, whom he accused of wearing "the clothes of Islam but are not Muslims" (Wedeen 1999, 48). The Muslim Brothers had been strongly opposed to the Alawites ever since the 1963 coup brought the Alawite-dominated Baath to power. Then, provoked by Asad's 1976 intervention on behalf of Maronite Christians in the Lebanese Civil War and his support of the Shiite regime of the Iranian Ayatollah Khomeini three years later, they carried out systematic acts of vio-

The martyr Basil ascending to the heavens.

(below) UNESCO photograph of Hafiz Asad's name inscribed on the western minaret of the Umayyad Mosque.

lence against the Asad regime. In retaliation Asad made membership in the Muslim Brotherhood "a capital offense punishable by death, with the ratification of Law No. 49" (HRW/ME 1996, 8).

Hama was the heart of Sunni Syria. From 1963, often from the pulpit, the Muslim Brothers coordinated urban uprisings. Many were thrown into prison, most in the infamous desert prison of Tadmor. The poet Faraj Bairaqdar (b. 1951), who was imprisoned there in 1987 on suspicion of membership in the Party for Communist Action and not released until November 2000, called Tadmor the "kingdom of death and madness." It is near the tourist site of Palmyra, with its five-star Cham Palace Hotel. In June 1980 some Muslim Brothers made an attempt on Asad's life. Vengeance came quickly. Commando forces from "the Defense Brigades and the 138th Security Brigade were helicoptered to the prison [of Tadmor] and murdered prisoners in their dormitories" (HRW/ME 1996, 8). It is estimated that between 250 and 500 Muslim Brothers were killed.

Then, in February 1982, after an outbreak of violence in Hama, Asad authorized the destruction of the old city of Hama, where Sunni militants were based. Invading the old city, military forces killed thousands. They razed much of the residential quarter to the ground and destroyed several *norias*, the Roman water wheels on the Orontes River that runs through the heart of Hama. Later the government built another five-star Cham Palace Hotel on part of the razed city, leaving a line of foundation stones two to three feet high along the sweeping drive to the entrance to remind and warn. Muslim Brothers who survived were incarcerated in Tadmor along with other political prisoners (chapter 7).

A few praised Asad for succeeding where other leaders had failed to curb their Islamist problem. Most remained shocked at the violence of the operation and the presumption of the president to kill Muslims in the name of an Islam that he claimed to embody.[10] For almost twenty years "events in Hama were only whispered about. But since September 11, things have changed, and Syria is seeking to repackage its experience in asphyxiating Muslim extremism as a textbook anti-terrorism campaign" (MacFarquhar 2002).

However crushed the Sunni opposition may have appeared to out-

Noria, or Roman water wheel, in Hama.

siders, Hafiz Asad was not convinced that he had effectively and finally dealt with the problem. In an interview with his biographer Patrick Seale, he said, "We were not just dealing with killers inside Syria, but with those who masterminded their plans. The plot thickened after Sadat's visit to Jerusalem (1978) and many foreign intelligence services became involved. Those who took part in Camp David used the Muslim Brothers against us" (Seale 1989, 335). The Hama massacre set the tone for the remainder of Asad's paranoid rule. More and more intellectuals who dared to speak their minds were detained, some for years without charge.[11]

The critical moment for Asad was the one with which I began: the fall of the Berlin Wall. In 1989 not just the Berlin Wall but also the socialist dictatorships of Eastern Europe collapsed. Asad had aligned himself with the Soviet Union and its European satellites to withstand the might of the United States in the region. The uprisings in Romania sounded the alarm in a country grown weary of the "heavy-handedness of the regime's rhetoric and with the cult of personality in which it is embedded. . . . Enough Syrians recognized the similarities between Asad and Romania's Nicolae Ceausescu to view the latter's fall as offering a potential blueprint for Syria's path to political liberalization" (Heydemann 1999, 2). The overthrow of Ceausescu and the "breakdown of the Eastern European single-party systems and the increasing role of democracy and human rights in western political discourse" must have persuaded Asad that it was time to soften his autocratic image in order to deflect local revolutionary ambitions (Lobmeyer 1994, 82, 88).

The Asad regime scrambled to distance itself from the failure of socialism in Eastern Europe. The government crafted a veneer of freedom and democracy. "In 1991 Asad announced that he had been converted to the free-enterprise system" (Johnson 1995, 85). It even allowed international agencies like Human Rights Watch and Amnesty International to conduct fact-finding missions that included attendance at staged trials. The irony is that these trials allowed the minister of justice, Hussein Hasun, and the minister of state for foreign affairs, Nassir Qadur, to declare that there was "no one in prison for belief or political action" (HRW 1991, 19).[12]

Even while the state let up on some fronts, it cracked down on others. The authorities were right to worry; the European revolutions were inspiring. Already in the last days of 1989 "graffiti appeared in Damascus referring to the Syrian president as *Shamsescu*.[13] Asad's response to the Eastern European events was three-pronged: first, to bring home to his people that Syria could not be compared to the states of the socialist bloc; second, to make clear the limits of opposition and demands for change he would tolerate; and, third, to mollify public discontent with a token relaxation of political control" (Perthes 1994, 65). But this "relaxation of political control" was indeed only token, since it took place under the omnipresent slogan *Qa'iduna ila al-abad al-amin*, or Our Leader into a Secure Eternity.

Many decided to leave the eternal security of Hafiz Asad's Syria because, like a character in a story by prison writer Ibrahim Samu'il (b. 1951), they could no longer stand "to meet in streets and alleys like thieves. . . . Nothing is going to change here, [anything is] better than dying here the way they please. . . . The country has become like . . . a nice hell" (1990, 58–60).

What is more significant is that others chose to stay and to go on creating even if that led to being "extinguished in the damp of prison cells" (Wannus 1996, 585). Many of the intellectuals I met during my six months in Damascus were playing a visible and often controversial role in the production of mid-1990s Syrian culture. Working within and against official definitions of good citizenship and patriotism, they hoped to evade charges of both treason and complicity (chapter 4). For them "the real struggle is inside" (*Index on Censorship* 1984, vol. 5, no. 18), where a space for dialogue among the citizens had to be created. They boldly questioned the power discourse and demanded accountability in order to incite others to do the same. Yet they remain largely unknown because few have been translated, and Syria continues to be a closed society. "Our literature does not leave our country," I was told again and again (chapter 2).

It is these creative dissidents who fought for freedom and struggled against hypocrisy who are the subject of this book. It is my hope that *Dissident Syria* will help Syrian culture leave the country and circulate so that it will no longer be so easy to say that a government and its ruler are the same as the people, that Hafiz Asad is the same as the Syrians.

The evidence of Syrian dissidence puts the lie to those who see only the public profile of a rogue state. In his acceptance speech for the 1950 Nobel Prize in Literature William Faulkner summed up the courage, creativity, and hope that I heard and read and saw in Syria between 1995 and 1996: "It is [the poet's, the writer's] privilege is to help man endure by lifting his heart, by reminding him of the courage and honor and hope and pride and compassion and pity and sacrifice which have been the glory of his past."[14]

What do you expect of a citizen who
for years and years has watched lorry-loads
of values, and slogans and speeches pass by
with each driver following his own whim
and direction?
—MUHAMMAD MAGHUT,
I Shall Betray My Homeland

chapter one

"CULTURE IS HUMANITY'S

HIGHEST NEED"

At the end of May 1996, I was to give a talk at the French Institute in Damascus. I had chosen for my title a slogan I'd seen scrawled on walls all over the Syrian capital: "Culture Is Humanity's Highest Need." The talk would give me an opportunity to try out some preliminary ideas about 1990s fiction and film and to check audience reactions to what I had to say about intellectual dissidence in Hafiz Asad's Syria.

The more I learned, however, the more puzzled I became. After living in Damascus for several months and talking with writers and filmmakers about their experiences in this police state, I was beginning to understand how complicated cultural production was. The contradiction between the official emphasis on culture and the stifling atmosphere in which intellectuals functioned seemed impossible to negotiate.

Struck by the popularity of the slogan "Culture Is Humanity's Highest Need" I had at first thought it would be safe to use. With time, however, I started to worry. What did it actually mean? How did Syrians read these words? What would they think of an American woman using this title to talk about dissident culture inside Syria?

Culture was a major preoccupation of the state. The Ministry of Culture encouraged writing, painting, sculpting, and filmmaking; it sponsored art shows and exhibitions of all sorts. Every day, the newspapers carried articles about the various cultural events happening in Damascus and elsewhere. Yet artists and writers secretly complained that they could scarcely breathe. They never knew when they were breaking the rules, were never sure about the consequences of what they did. What had been allowed yesterday might not be tomorrow, and one intellectual might be punished for expressing mild dissent while another, more vocal, would get away with explicit criticism. Daily, they had to negotiate the permissible, assuming a responsibility that might cost them their freedom and even their lives. How were they able to survive inside the country while "living in truth"?

As If . . .

To live in truth, according to the Czech dissident playwright and later president Vaclav Havel, entails assuming "responsibility to and for the whole." The attempt to live in truth often brings intellectuals and writers up against oppressive regimes. In their struggle against the status quo they hope to create conditions that will allow for the emergence "of the independent life of society (where) free thought, alternative values and 'alternative behaviour' can exist and exert pressure" (1987, 104–105). The voices of intellectuals living in truth, especially when such living is not easy, need to be magnified (Rushdie 2005).

Reading Havel's influential "Power of the Powerless," a 1978 manifesto against the official manipulation of public signs and symbols in socialist Czechoslovakia, struck a chord as I looked around Asad's Syria. Like pre-1989 Eastern Europe, the technology of Syria's Soviet-style socialist regime depended on a rhetoric that was "permeated with hypocrisy and lies. . . . The complete degradation of the individual is presented as his or her ultimate liberation; depriving people of information is called making it available . . . the repression of culture is called its development . . . the lack of free expression becomes the highest form of freedom . . . military occupation becomes fraternal assistance. . . . Because the regime is captive to its own lies, it must falsify everything. . . . It pretends to pretend nothing" (1987, 44).

Havel's depiction of life in socialist Czechoslovakia may overstate the case for turn-of-the-century Syria, yet he does provide a useful framework for the examination of the Asad cult. The regime's manipulation of meanings to buttress the cult of the president established the ground rules for behavior in a political culture where the rhetoric was manifestly unbelievable. But real belief was not the issue in Syria, just as it had not been in Eastern Europe. For Havel individuals "need not believe all these mystifications, but they must behave *as though* they did, or they must at least tolerate them in silence, or get along well with those who work with them. For this reason, however, they must *live within a lie*. They need not accept the lie. It is enough for them to have accepted their life with it and in it. For by this very fact, individuals confirm the system, fulfill the system, make the system, *are* the system" (1987, 45; my emphasis).

State sloganeering and the public response to it in pre-1989 Eastern Europe illuminates the situation in mid-1990s Syria: arbitrary abuse of power; the repression of culture dubbed its development; and proscribed speech and writing translated into the highest form of freedom. Havel's offhand "military occupation becomes fraternal assistance" described Syria's 1976 military occupation of Lebanon during its civil war, an occupation that was coded assistance for "our brothers." The regime was captive to its own lies.

"Don't trust any politicians," said the former minister of defense Mustafa Tlas in a disarmingly frank interview, "they all lie. They have

مرحبا بكم في القرداحة .. عرين القائد الأسد

Asad posters on a highway overpass.

to lie otherwise they would not stay in power" (Koelbl 2005, 114). And those who behave as if they believe such lies are themselves living within a lie.

Havel's urban landscape draped with party banners painted the panorama of Syrian cities hung with huge posters of President Asad, some with his two sons, Basil (the car crash martyr) and Bashar (the current president). To endure the public displays of personal power, the people seemed oblivious to the banners bearing the ideology of the Corrective Movement. It was as if the messages pressing in on them did not get through, as if, like pre-1989 Czechs, they "do what is done, what is to be done, what must be done, but at the same time—by that very token—they confirm that it must be done in fact.

They conform to a particular requirement and, in so doing, they themselves perpetuate that requirement" (Havel 1987, 51).

Ibrahim Samu'il's "People . . . People" illustrates this performative complicity with a terrible system that the people resented but refused to confront. In this short story, passengers are angry with a bus driver who once again is deliberately reckless, and they mutter complaints under their breath. Finally someone plucks up the courage to protest aloud, assuming that he is speaking the mind of the people. To his dismay, the passengers turn on him, yelling that the last thing they need is a philosopher or a lawyer. They kick him off the bus, which rages into the distance wilder than ever. Standing in the cold, he watches them hold on to each other in terror, anxiously awaiting "the moment of liberation when they reach their stop" (1990, 13). The moral of the story is clear: those who courageously expose the tyranny of the system should not expect thanks. Not only the regime but also the people will punish such dissidence. It is so much easier, after all, to act as if nothing's wrong.

Even when they know they could rebel most prefer not to. It is easier to submit to the system, however painful. In "Buq'at al-daw'" (A spot of light) 'Abd al-Salam al-'Ujayli, a medical doctor and writer from Raqqa, writes about a prisoner in solitary confinement in pitch darkness who must keep his hands held above his head. With time he realizes that he need not always hold his hands aloft. All he has to do is keep an eye on the tiny spot of light that comes through the door when the guard is not blocking it; only then must he raise his arms. With time, however, staring at the spot becomes so intolerable that he prefers "to bear whatever befalls me so long as I am free of this torture" (1987, 93–94). It is easier to be absolutely obedient than to remain constantly alert and vigilant and terrified.

In her analysis of the political climate of Asad's Syria in the 1980s and 1990s Wedeen asserts convincingly that Syrians probably recognized the disparity between their experiences and the empty claims and promises attendant upon the cult. Yet they continued to act *as if* they believed, and in so doing they perpetuated the system. Power did not depend on people's belief in this discourse but only on their performance of belief and their resulting entanglement in "self-enforcing relations of domination" (1999, 84; see also 6, 68, 76–77, 131, 145).

It is this numbed tolerance of mystifications that Havel denounced because it creates a coercive norm (1987, 52). Writing twenty-five years after the publication of "Power of the Powerless," the Slovenian cultural critic Slavoj Žižek explains that Havel's notion of living in truth "involves no metaphysics of truth or authenticity; it simply designates the act of suspending one's participation in the game. . . . Havel mercilessly cuts off and denounces all false modes of distance towards the ruling ideology. . . . Such acts of indifference, of making fun of official rituals in private circles, are the very mode of reproduction of the official ideology. . . . The greatest catastrophe for the regime would have been for its own ideology to be taken seriously" (2001, 91–92). It is not enough not to believe in the lies to live in truth; to act as if the ruling ideology can be distanced through disbelief serves the regime: it reproduces the ideology through its performance. Havel's notion of living in truth entails paying attention to the power discourse and rejecting its falsifications. It was only when intellectuals suspended their participation in the power game that they could address the world and show "everyone that it is possible to live within the truth" (Havel 1987, 56).

This is what the Damascus University philosopher Ahmad Barqawi did in a talk he gave at the Asad Library during the Asad Book Fair in September 1995. I had gone with some friends to listen to him lecture on the "Consciousness of Freedom." Freedom, Barqawi boldly announced, "only exists when we become conscious of slavery. This consciousness demands change in a society that deprives individuals of their right to fight for freedom." He did not mention the president directly, but who else was he designating in his criticism of a society that deprives individuals of their right to fight for freedom? Again and again, he threw out to his audience Albert Camus's challenge: "Ana atamarrad idhan ana mawjud" (I rebel therefore I am).[1] The people should not be duped into believing that they are free when they are not. I heard his words as a call to action, to suspend participation in the as-if game lest they continue to be slaves. They should beware the "false consciousness" of freedom, because "freedom is never total.

It is an on-going, evolving and sometimes painful process. Democracies defend individuals' right to engage in the process." Was this "false consciousness of freedom" not a reference to the as-if behavior that Havel condemned? Barqawi seemed to be pointing to the complicity of Syrians who know they are not free but who act as if they believe the power discourse that tells them they are. Thus understood, his reference to "individuals' right to engage in the process" meant suspending their participation in the power game in order to liberate the real meaning of freedom and thus make the regime accountable for its rhetoric. He ended his talk by warning, "Time takes revenge on systems that deprive individuals of their freedom." Barqawi published a version of this speech four years later in the Lebanese journal *Al-Adab*, where he elaborated on his argument for freedom, writing, "The people can only produce representative authority if they are free and enjoy their rights and perform their duties. Freedom can only be expressed through political parties. And the free citizen can only come into being with the shattering of the old systems" (1999, 52). During six months in Damascus I heard other intellectuals utter that very threat.

Listening to Barqawi's fiery speech only a month after my arrival in Damascus, I was amazed. But friends who had taken me to the book fair and to the lecture were nonplussed by my reaction. Didn't I know that freedom is enshrined in the state constitution, along with unity and socialism?[2] Had I not read the Arab Writers Union statement that promises writers freedom? I hadn't, but when I did I was struck by the way it referred to censorship: "Their only censor will be their conscience and their commitment to the principles undergirding the nation. [Individual commitment] cannot be separated from commitment to one's country and society. . . . The writers and artists who produce the greatest works are those who realize this link in its highest form. They are at once free and committed" (Arab Writers Union 1978, 31, 35–37). In other words, their conscience and their commitment to the principles undergirding the nation were their only censors.

Not quite! In a 1990 interview, a Syrian censor who defected and used the pseudonym Adib Sadiq, or Truthful Writer, asserted that

Asad had transformed the whole state structure into "one large intelligence and censorship apparatus" (*Index on Censorship* June 1987, 26). The media, he explained, had to be controlled because it shaped public opinion: "The philosophy directed at the media supposes that the people have no demands and no interests aside from the demands and interests of the regime. . . . The practical goal of the media's activity is to prevent any consensus on a popular level, even a consensus that suits the regime, because the system is based on limiting politics to the highest decision-making body centre and on removing it as far as possible from the people" (Sadiq 1990, 20–21). Censorship was calibrated in such a way that it maintained tension and suspicion. Its goal was atomism. Promotion in journalism depended on writing secret reports about acquaintances, friends, and even family. So dire was the situation in the early 1990s that a lawyer, who refused to identify himself, claimed that he had "witnessed trials where the only crime was reading the newspaper of an opposition political party and the sentence was fifteen years" (15).

Above all, censorship was arbitrary. Even if writers internalized the unwritten rules and what they wrote had been officially approved, they might find themselves retroactively censored (Sadiq 1990, 21). Consequently, not only writers but also censors lived in constant dread because if they allowed what was no longer permissible they, too, were liable to punishment (HRW 1991, 124). Stringent control extended to the international press. While I was in Damascus the *International Herald Tribune* was often late; sometimes a week passed before the newspaper reached the stalls with sections inked out (see HRW 1991, 109, 123).

Slogans, Slogans Everywhere

A couple of weeks before giving the scheduled talk at the French Institute, I met with a teacher at the Institute and a leading intellectual who, I later was told, had the power to make or break upcoming talent. He was to "animate" my seminar; in other words, he would introduce me and then lead the discussion. He was quite gruff.

"Are you still going to use that title: 'Culture Is Humanity's Highest Need'?"

"Yes, it's a bit late to change it, isn't it? Hasn't it been advertised?"

The slogan was everywhere, so why shouldn't I use it? During the September 1995 Asad annual book fair, where Ahmad Barqawi had spoken so passionately about freedom and the price to be paid for its denial, the slogan was all over the Stalinesque building that looms over the Umayyad Square. Again in November, during the twenty-five-year celebrations of the Corrective Movement, the streets outside the Ministry of Culture were draped with cloth banners bearing the slogan. All cultural events were held under the auspices of the Ministry of Culture, and during that festive period Minister Najah al-'Attar would send huge bouquets of gladioli or whatever large flowers happened to be in season with the slogan laced through the leaves.

Where did the words come from? I asked 'Ali al-Qayim, deputy to the minister of culture. He had just written a report on the very subject and he gave me a copy.[3] The ministry, he confided, was planning its annual strategy around this phrase. Apparently, the president had made the statement in 1984 during the inauguration of the Asad Library. In fact, he had written on the opening page of the guest book, "Culture is humanity's highest need [Al-thaqafa hiya al-haja al-a'la [sic] li-al-bashariya]. All existential human needs have their limits, except for the cultural need which has no limits." I went to the library to see the guest book. I was apprehensive that the librarian would find my request inappropriate, but my fears were groundless. In fact, she was pleased to be asked and led me to a gold plaque inscribed with the words the president had penned back in 1984. Then she showed me the book and gave me a photocopy of the page with Hafiz Asad's signature.

So "culture," like "freedom," was a good word, one that the state liked to use, to hear, and to see. But why would a military dictatorship place such an emphasis on culture? What did this word, *thaqafa*, mean? In Lane's *Arabic-English Lexicon* the noun contains much of the vagueness and contestation inherent in the English word, whereas the verb, especially in its causative derived form, *thaqqafa*,

Photocopy of the Asad Library guest book with "Culture is humanity's highest need" in Hafiz Asad's handwriting.

is unambiguously disciplinary. It means "he disciplined him, or educated him well, and amended him, or improved him" and, most interestingly, "straightened what was crooked."

What did the noun thaqafa mean to Hafiz Asad and to his officials who reverently quoted his words? Were they using the term in an aesthetic or an anthropological sense? Were they using it the way the Saudi dissident in exile in Syria 'Abd al-Rahman Munif (1940–2004) defined it to articulate the historical consciousness of the age? For

Munif, culture is a "realistic awareness of dangers and challenges through which the hopes for the future may be read. . . . It is a set of basic and evolving values focused primarily on principles of truth, justice, freedom and honor. . . . It entails resistance to injustice whatever its source. . . . Excessive sloganeering about total unity and socialism is the accoutrement of inherently military systems that eliminate political parties, fetter the press and destroy civil society at its core" (1993, 12, 18). It seemed unlikely that this was the state's understanding of culture since this definition exposes slogans and articulates the spirit of the age in terms of a struggle for truth, justice, and freedom. Culture shapes, and is shaped by, its people. Perhaps the state's understanding of culture was connected to *muthaqqaf*, the Arabic for "intellectual." For critic Mustafa Dandashli the intellectual is someone whose "critical, contestatory discourse . . . encourages change through literature and discourse . . . [and] helps society to become self-conscious. . . . Culture is a theoretical, practical and programmatic consciousness concerning society. . . . Intellectuals today have a particularly important role in liberating the land, the country and the people" (1996, 76–78). This definition of culture that emphasizes the revolutionary role of intellectuals echoes the state's definition. If intellectuals are so important, the state has to control them in order to control the people.

Control of intellectuals in order to control the people is no simple matter. Terry Eagleton is surely right to point out that "no political power can survive satisfactorily by naked coercion. . . . But in order to secure the consent of those it governs, it needs to know them more intimately than as a set of graphs or statistical tables. . . . If it is to regulate them from the inside, it must also imagine them from the inside. And no cognitive form is more adroit at mapping the complexities of the heart than artistic culture" (2000, 36, 50). Here the political is imbricated with the aesthetic. Culture is a way for the state to infiltrate individuals' consciousness, to get to know them, with their hopes and their fears, and to shape their thinking without naked coercion. In other words, just as culture needs the state for support and distribution, so the state needs culture to legitimate and extend its power.

From the perspective of the state, culture can become a technology of social control, the management of meaning and the construction of a symbolic universe in the service of ideology, whose social function, according to James H. Kavanagh, is not to give knowledge "but to constitute, adjust, and/or transform social subjects. The distinctive effect of ideology is not theatrical but pragmatic, to enable various social subjects to feel at home, and to act (or not act), within the limits of a given social project" (1990, 314). And in Syria, ideology as culture served the Asad cult. Just as in English, "culture" is tied to its cognate, "cult,"[4] so in Arabic culture/thaqafa is connected to the disciplinarity of thaqqafa, the verbal causative form meaning "to straighten crookedness." Culture in the service of the cult entails educating, improving, and, above all, straightening what is crooked in the citizens. Culture in Syria was linked to the cult of the president.

That was why the regime had to control the symbolic universe its citizens inhabited: so that the cult should thrive. The regime, like pre-1989 Romania, "strove to suppress alternative messages and capture 'ears,' crucial to gaining the resources that would facilitate a broader hearing for their message" (Verdery 1991, 12). Such alternative messages are found in films, literature, and art; they are powerful because they reflect, frame, and shape an interpretive community. That is why the state strove to appropriate these messages to create its own cultural capital and why intellectuals had to craft their art so that it would escape this management while challenging the state.

Freedom and Democracy

In plays, films, and fiction, writers like the poet Muhammad Maghut have parodied the lying rhetoric of the regime and its penchant for slogans.[5] In his 1987 *I Shall Betray My Homeland*, Maghut urges readers to search for the truth, acknowledge it, and then live in it. He is unequivocal in denouncing the empty rhetoric of Arab Nationalism, Freedom, Steadfastness, and Honor, calling these words, when they are mindlessly repeated, "ammunition in the Israeli arsenal" (2001, 157). Those who mouth these words become the system. They repeat slogans because they feel they are being watched, and in order to prove their patriotism they watch others. That is how the system works; each person watches and is watched: "Yes, my friend, here the intelligence agents watch each other; the students watch each other; the writers watch each other," and so on for twenty-two categories of persons who must watch and be watched, twenty-two groups internally monitored under a government that watches the people while the people watch the government. And then above the people and the government is Israel, which watches but is not watched (52). In their enthusiasm to prove their patriotism, individuals undercut each other, forgetting how alert Israel remains to moments of vulnerability. In their absorption with the as-if game, both the regime and the people open themselves up to the greatest danger of all: Israel.

Those who shout and clap and hurtle along with a party agenda they do not understand, or care to understand, risk falling into the Israeli trap. They are like the speeding driver who responds to the policeman with slogans:

"Why were you speeding?"

"To catch up with events."

"Your ID?"

"From the Ocean to the Gulf." (This is a popular designation for the Arab world, which stretches from the Atlantic Ocean to the Arabian Gulf.)

"We want your name and full details."

"Register: I am an Arab," he says, quoting the famous line of poetry from the Palestinian poet Mahmud Darwish that every Palestinian child learns with her first words. "I live where the independence battles are being fought."

Told to be more specific, the driver launches into a list of forty-seven landmarks along the way home: streets, schools, political party headquarters, government offices, trade unions, and then shops, theaters, and public gardens, each boasting the name of an independence hero or a battle or the name of one of the thousands of conferences or summits convened to strengthen Arab unity and solidarity, the emptiest of all the many empty signifiers. Then, at the end of the last road and the last slogan affixed to the last street sign or building or garden is the Israeli Embassy that watches everyone (Maghut 2001, 205–207).

So many are the causes bandied about, so ubiquitous the slogans that even those who have paid the heaviest price may not know which cause they have defended. Take the mother who did not know on whose behalf her son had died. Some told her that he was a martyr for the revolution in Chad, others that he had died to defeat the conspiracy in Lebanon or to protect the Arabness of the Gulf. Cause after great cause, "yet all his mother knows is that they brought him home hastily wrapped in various flags" (Maghut 2001, 165). Well, she muses, no matter the cause, with the money earned from the sweat of her brow she would build him a splendid grave inscribed with Qur'anic verses and great poetry. But when she felt for the bundle of money tucked in her blouse she could not find it. Thunderstruck, she collapsed on the pavement. Somewhere else, two passengers from the same bus on which she had been riding "were opening a paltry peasant's bundle and counting out its contents" (166). In such a system, the greatest sacrifice is without value.

Many of the poem-essays in *I Shall Betray My Homeland* read like a police file. Only this time it is the civilian who is recording the evidence, sometimes against the government(s), sometimes against fellow countrymen, and, sometimes, against himself, but never against the leader. Maghut begs God to grant him "the stupidity of geese so that I might believe what I see and the innocence of Joan of Arc to believe what I hear and see" (2001, 210). He needs help in learning the as-if game. In the meantime, maybe God will grant him and all the children of the East spiders' legs so that they might dangle from the ceiling of the homeland until this period of sloganeering and terror should pass. The people are like prisoners in a concentration camp who have no idea how much strength they have in their numbers. Echoing Barqawi, Maghut encourages the people to take the freedom slogan at its word just once and even if only for one day. Then, he promises, "you will see how great are your people and how small is Israel" (86).

But everyone, the state and the people, fears freedom. Consider the average conference where Arab unity, solidarity, and honor are studied, recommendations are adopted, and committees are formed. Topic after topic is tackled and "solved" until it comes to freedom. At that point the chair stands up and "sticks a long piece of tape over each person's mouth, saying: 'Now let's discuss freedom in the Arab homeland" (Maghut 2001,135–148). Arab Unity, Palestine, and Honor can be discussed freely; recommendations that will never be implemented can be proposed. But freedom is something else; it can be negotiated only with mouths taped shut.

An artistic rendering of mouth taping can be found in Hasan 'Abbas and Ahmad Maala's *Citizenship Guide* (2005). The extraordinary guide to citizens' rights to life and freedom consists of alternating pages of text by 'Abbas and images of clay figures by Maala. In their ironic and often contradictory juxtaposition, the images and the text highlight not the citizens' rights but rather their systematic violation. In this case, the image that faces the text entitled "The duty to bear witness in court" (67) is a face with its mouth taped shut. The text insists on the individual's duty, but also her right, to be heard; indeed, "it is a crime to keep silent." But the image then challenges the text: How can a citizen do her duty without committing the sin of silence because her mouth is taped shut?

Mouths must be taped when it comes to bearing witness to the truth in court and when discussing freedom because truth and freedom evoke their opposite. The poet Faraj Bairaqdar explains how this works: freedom is not fully experienced except in confinement. While he was in prison he "wrote a lot about freedom. . . . Even when a country is occupied its free citizens can liberate it. But when they are cowed into slavery they cannot free themselves. We have lots of splendid slogans and encomia to our noble, free country. We are supposed to deduce that the citizens are free. But the reality is prisons, prisoners and everlasting martial law" (Jundi 2005). Here and in other poetry anthologies, including *You Are Not Alone* (1979), *Jalsarkhi* (1981), and *The Free-winged Dove* (1997), those prisons and prisoners mirror the confinement of daily life in Syria, a confinement grown ordinary.

Maghut suggests that because of its long suppression, freedom has become repulsive. Even if freedom were to "come knocking at my

"The Duty to Bear Witness in Court." In Abbas and Maala, *Citizenship Guide* (2005), p. 66.

door one stormy night when I was sick in bed and it were to say in its commanding voice: Open up! It's me, Freedom! Would I believe it so easily? Of course not . . . who can prove that it really is freedom. I've never heard its voice nor seen its shape or color or texture. So, I'll just slam the door in its face and chase it away like the old peasant woman chases away the hen that does not belong in her farm" (2001, 326).

Maghut's exposé of the emptiness of slogans forced me to go back to the slogan I had chosen for my French Institute talk: "Culture Is Humanity's Highest Need." The slogan was not mere rhetoric. It was a very real and necessary part of the government agenda that translated "repression of culture" into "its development," to paraphrase Havel. Because culture is an urgent human need it has to be repressed, or at the very least "straightened from its crookedness." Only then can it serve the Asad cult.

The key to understanding the slogan is to think about what it omits: subject, verb, and object. The slogan does not say *who* is going to *do what to whom* about this urgent human need. The missing subject was the state that distributed the slogan around town, the state that was concerned with this universal need. Once the state enters the slogan as subject, culture/cult becomes its means, and the people its object. We can now follow Havel's analysis of the word "culture" for socialist Czechoslovakia: the state is going to develop culture by repressing it and straightening its crookedness into the cult. The assumption that culture must be *developed* because it is humanity's highest need is where the lie is to be found. It is the assumption that is wrong, not the slogan. Precisely because culture is humanity's highest need, it must be repressed, and the repression is covered by its enthusiastic repetition. Power works in the interstices of repression and repetition.

In May I gave the talk at the French Institute, and I focused on women and their role in constructing Syrian culture.

chapter two

OUR LITERATURE DOES NOT LEAVE

THE COUNTRY

I had come to Syria to meet its women writers, not knowing what I might find. Even specialists of Arabic literature did not know much about the cultural scene inside Hafiz Asad's Syria of the 1990s. Many assumed that such a regime is so repressive that writers of conscience are either in jail, like Faraj Bairaqdar, or in exile, like Zakaria Tamer (b. 1931) and many, many others. In 1992, the critic Jean Fontaine reduced the whole of Syrian literature to nightmare, "overwhelmed by a sense of betrayal. How could it be otherwise in a climate devoid of freedom of expression, where there are no intermediaries between the people and the state?" (1992, 110). Were women writing inside Syria?

I had long known two Syrian women writers who had left Damascus in the 1960s to settle in Beirut. Ghada Samman (b. 1942) is one of the Arab world's best-known fiction writers, and Houda Naamani (b. 1930) is a Sufi poet. I had met them just after graduate school, in the summer of 1980 in Beirut, where I was researching a book on Lebanese civil war literature.

I got Ghada Samman's telephone number from a friend and called her at home. The author of more than twenty books, including novels and mostly absurdist short stories and some poetry, she could be quite unpredictable, people told me. To my surprise and relief she was very friendly on the phone and agreed to meet me.

"How about tonight?" Samman offered. "Let's have dinner at Pasha's!"

Tonight? But there's a curfew! Pooh-poohing my nervousness, she said she'd pick me up from my Clemenceau apartment at six. At the appointed time I waited for the doorbell to ring. Six-fifteen. Six-thirty. Still no Ghada. I paced back and forth from the balcony into the apartment and then out again, thinking all the while that it had been too good to be true. Finally, I took a good look at a car parked about a hundred meters down the road. Two men in caps standing next to it had not moved for the half hour that I had been going in and out of the apartment. I waved tentatively when I noticed one of them looking up at the balcony on which I was standing. He acknowledged my greeting and I rushed out, filled with apologies for having kept them waiting and wondering what had happened to Ghada. When I got to the car, the younger of the two men turned to me and, taking off his cap, let loose a mane of shining black hair. The comedy had started well!

Our dinner in the empty restaurant overlooking the Mediterranean, our food piled high and untouched, remains vivid in my mind. We talked of the war, of her education in London, and why she had chosen to study the theater of the absurd, of my interest in women's writings about the Lebanese civil war, of everything except her recent war writings.

"What do owls signify in your work?"

She had chosen an owl for the logo of her publishing house that Bashir Daouk, her husband and owner of the famous publishing house Al-Talia, had just established. Owls figured in several of her stories.

"Owls? Nothing. Why do you ask? Kaasik, cheers."

A round of arak.

"Were the nightmares in *Beirut Nightmares* [1976] ones you had when you were caught in the crossfire?"

Her villa had been in the neighborhood that opposing militias had occupied during the famous Battle of the Hotels in November 1976. In hundreds of vignettes that she calls nightmares she evokes the terror and absurdity of a few days spent cowering in corners and fantasizing wildly.

"What do you mean? The novel's not about me. You know, you're never going to write about me. But I will write about you."

Well, I did and she didn't. That was the only time I saw her during my two extended stays in Beirut during the summers of 1980 and 1982. But we kept in touch. Years later, we met in Paris, where she had gone when things deteriorated even further. We toasted our first meeting and laughed about how much arak we had drunk and how little we had eaten.

Houda Naamani was quite another matter. Our first meeting was in her antiques-filled apartment in a building on the green line dividing East and West Beirut. She welcomed me warmly and introduced me to her husband, an older man in a wheelchair. She had left Damascus for Cairo as a teenager with her new husband, and later they established their home in Beirut. Her dark eyes always about to overflow with tears of tenderness or sparks of passion, Houda invited me at once into the world of her imagination and poetry: violence and God, hatred and love, and a butterfly escaping its cocoon to flutter high above the desolation that was Beirut. She read me her poems out loud and laughed with childlike pleasure when I told her how much I liked them. Her epic poem *I Remember I Was a Point I Was a Circle* (1978) sought a spiritual resolution to what the politicians and their minions refused to end.

She invited me to her place often and we would study her poems together, trying to translate some of them into English. We might spend thirty minutes on one word, probing its meaning and mystical resonances to render it in an English that, no matter how hard we tried, was always flat-footed.

After 1983, the U.S. government banned travel to Lebanon and I could not return until the spring of 2002. During the 1980s, we met twice in London, where she was visiting her son, Lebanon's ambassador to the Court of King James. She told me of the terrible years she had spent in that apartment. Yet even these dark years had their moments of light. One day, militiamen came and told her to leave because they were about to occupy the building. Houda refused. I imagined her standing in the doorway to her dark apartment, her black hair wild around her defiant eyes, legs firmly planted, mouth set tight.

"Who are you?" one of the militiamen asked.

"I am Houda Naamani."

"The poet?"

To her amazement, the churlish fellow pulled a crumpled piece of paper out of his uniform pocket and shyly showed her one of her poems. She was allowed to stay, and the crazy young men took special care of her while the bullets whizzed to and from her building. And in the hell that this peaceful place must have become, she went on writing her poems, her supplications to God to stay with Lebanon. Surely it was during those days that she wrote *Houda . . . I Am Thy Lord* (1991), a lyrical meditation on her relationship with a god that is not so much the transcendent deity of Islam as a deeply personal, universal spirit. Watching the Armenian painter Gregorian illustrate her poem inspired her to experiment in art, and she threw herself into painting with the same passion that drove her poetic creations.

Nadia al-Ghazzi

Yes, I knew these two expatriate Syrian writers. But who was writing inside Syria? During my first week in Damascus in August 1995, I ran into Houda quite by chance. I was walking up Abu Rummana, the street that cuts through the diplomatic district toward one of

Hafiz Asad's palaces and beyond to Mount Qasyun, when I heard my name. It was Houda, who happened to be in town for two days with her daughter-in-law. What was I doing for lunch? She would like to introduce me to her cousin Nadia who was also a writer. My work had started.

Nadia al-Ghazzi (b. 1935) was a lawyer with her own legal practice who wrote on the side. She lived three blocks from our apartment, so I walked to her place. The apartment was elegant but stiffly formal, as though no one lived there. Nadia had lost her husband to cancer two years earlier and she was still grieving. Sadness had settled into the folds of the curtains and in the corners of the rooms. It made every conversation seem trivial. But Nadia was eager to talk.

She told me about her family: her father, who had been prime minister during the presidency of Shukri al-Quwatli in the early days of Syria's independence, and her mother, who had danced with Ataturk when she was fourteen. Then, in 1964, the Baath regime expropriated most of their vast landholdings. They had lost everything except for a charming farm in Rayhan, an hour outside Damascus, not far from the regional capital of Douma. There she was transformed from the wistful widow I had first met into an excited teenager who rushed around the house and garden, smelling the roses and arranging elaborate picnics. One day, she invited me along with a group of women from the "old bourgeoisie." Over tea and fruit they talked about the good old days, their Turkish grandparents, and the lost world of courtly etiquette.

Nadia's legal work defending female clients for twenty years had provided her with ample material for her fiction. So real were the cases she detailed that some people complained that her stories were too close to theirs. In her writings, women criminals and victims brush up against abusive men. And it is these men, like the nurse in "Ward No. 6," whom she addresses. Men who think they can continue to abuse women with impunity will one day pay the price. The story ends with a little man hanging at the end of a rope, a warning to all violent men (al-Ghazzi 1989, 343–363).

No, none of her stories had been translated.

"Our literature never leaves the country."

This was the first time I heard this lament that others would repeat right up to my last day in Syria. This is why foreign critics like Jean Fontaine know so little about writing inside, and so they claim that Syrian literature is all the same, just one nightmare response to undifferentiated oppression. Such an attitude implied that it is all cathartic, not worth studying.

It may have been her awareness of cultural isolation that led Nadia to broaden her scope. In 1993, she published *Barhum's Baggy Pants* about the Safarbarlik, the forced mobilization of Syrian men to fight on behalf of the fading Ottoman Empire during World War I. While soldiers were struggling and barely surviving in places as distant as Yemen and Suez, their families were devastated by a famine at home. During the 1990s, several other Syrian writers, including the Alawite poet and playwright Mamduh 'Adwan, also wrote plays and fiction about the Safarbarlik. It provided a powerful allegory for their current situation. This time it was not only Nadia's clients who read her work, but also the critics. Some accused her of riding a bandwagon. But her novel was quite different from other renditions, like 'Adwan's *The Ghoul* (chapter 5).

Nadia al-Ghazzi wrote about an old peasant woman who had given a certain Shafiq al-Imam, chief administrator of the ancient Azm Palace, a pair of brightly colored, embroidered baggy pants:

I was a bride when they took my husband of a month to the military. . . . I was hoping that when he came home and all the loved ones greeted him he would be wearing a beautiful pair of baggy pants. So I bought the material and went to the fountain where I would sit and contemplate the colors of the flowers. Then I would embroider them on the baggy pants. Then the war ended. . . . And I waited. . . . I waited. . . . My groom did not return. . . . So I put these pants into a box. Whenever I missed him I would open the box and take out the pants and then return them just as they were. . . . This went on for forty years. . . . But now I'm sick and I need medicine and the most precious thing I own is this pair of baggy pants. . . . Will you buy them for a gold lira and a half? That's the price of the material and thread. I'm not asking anything for the embroidery work. (1993, 1)

Other Syrian women, such as Colette al-Khuri (b. 1937) and Ulfat Idilbi (b. 1918), were also writing historical novels set in the time of their grandfathers, when resistance to oppression was the order of the day. When I asked whether they might be pointing to revolutionary models in a safe, nationalistic period, Nadia dodged the question.

"Have you seen Marwan al-Masri and Muhammad ʿAli Waʾlani's compendium of Syrian women writers? There are more than a hundred. Even if a third don't write fiction, the list's impressive. There are many good writers, but you should definitely contact Colette and Ulfat" (see Masri and Waʾlani 1988).

That is the way it worked in Beirut in 1980 when I was researching women's literature of the civil war. I had arrived with two or three names, some with an address and telephone number. Each woman I met gave me two or three more names, until I had over fifty names and had met with at least half of the women. When al-Ghazzi urged me to get in touch with Colette and Ulfat, she was referring to Colette al-Khuri and Ulfat Idilbi. I knew their work from the 1950s and 1960s, but I had not read anything recent. I had no idea what they were doing or even if they were still alive. They were not only alive but also still very active.

Colette al-Khuri

I visited Colette al-Khuri in late September. Unlike other Damascene homes, al-Khuri's was less concerned with orderliness and self-presentation. Hers was full of books, strewn on shelves and piled high on the floor, and photographs, many of her. A huge bowl of foil-covered chocolates was balanced on some books. It was a comfortable space.

A pioneer of Arab feminism, she had written angry stories in the 1950s about men and their selfishness and unthinking misogyny. Her first novel, *Ayyam maʿahu* (Days with him, 1959), shocked the Arab world with its outspoken expression of a woman's sexuality and desire. At a time when Arab women were only beginning to awaken to a sense of violated rights, Colette created a strong woman whose love was not so overpowering that it blinded her to the weaknesses of her lover. Some did not like the fact that she was writing about her affair with the popular poet Nizar Qabbani.

Two years later, she published *Layla wahida* (One night, 1961), about the one night Rasha spent with the mysterious Kamal, a Syrian bomber pilot in the French air force during World War II. What matters is not that she gave Kamal her body but that she decided to whom to give it (al-Khuri 1992, 197). She was a rebel in a society where men's desire is lauded and women's desire denied.

Colette al-Khuri was one of the very first to put women on the literary agenda. But after the early 1960s no more was heard from her abroad. I assumed that she had stopped writing. But that was not the case. She had continued to write, even if not about women, and that, perhaps, is why she had lost her international readers.

When I met her she was putting the final touches on the second of five volumes about Faris al-Khuri, her grandfather who had been prime minister and had fought for independence from the French. The first two volumes of *Awraq Faris al-Khuri* (The papers of Faris al-Khuri) examine the years of his struggle against the Ottomans and their Safarbarlik from 1877 until 1918, and then the six years following the end of World War I, when the British and the French divided much of the Middle East between them. Colette comes from a notable family: her grandfather has become a folk hero for his resistance to the French, and her father had been minister for village and town affairs. It was no surprise, then, that she should also enter politics. Of twenty-four women members (and 226 men) of the Majlis al-Shaʿb, the Syrian People's Assembly, she was proud to be the only independent (though she never explained what that meant). One woman was a communist and the other twenty-two were "afraid of their own shadows."

When we talked about my earlier work on Lebanon she urged me to read *Ayyam maʿa al-ayyam* (Days upon days), a novel she set in 1960s Beirut, the capital of Arab dissidence at the time. She told me that she preferred this novel to her more famous first work, and she especially liked her "bourgeois" (a word she kept using) protagonist, for whom her country was more important than her leftist boyfriend and his tongue-deep patriotism.

Colette liked to talk politics. She was particularly proud of her special relationship with Hafiz Asad that went back to 1969. After a stint in Beirut, she was returning to Damascus when she was stopped at the border. The guard told her that Syria no longer wanted its bourgeois citizens. A quaint turn of phrase. Outraged, she called the minister of defense, Hafiz Asad, and he ordered the guard to let her through.

"Since then he has always called me his friend from the border," she beamed.

I wasn't sure how to reconcile pride in being the only independent in Parliament and pleasure in this friendship with the president. I was to learn that it was not at all uncommon to criticize everything in Syria while evincing admiration, even love, for Hafiz Asad. He was the rightly guided leader, and it was those corrupt officials around him who were responsible for anything that went wrong.

Colette al-Khuri was very patriotic. *Luminous Days* (1984) is a collection of stories about the glorious 1973 October War (see introduction).[1] It lionizes Syrians, such as a military surgeon who operates on an Israeli pilot just shot out of the sky. He comments ruefully that only a few hours earlier he had been ready to tear any Israeli from limb to limb: "Looks as though my wish has come true. . . . But we are a humane people. That's our greatness. When I saw this wounded man stretched out on the table I forgot the war and my feelings of vengeance. I remembered only that I was a doctor who had to help someone in need" (50).

When we next met I had a favor to ask. Anne Casper, the American cultural attaché, had asked me to organize a *nadwa*, or symposium, on Syrian women writers. I decided not to talk about the patriotic war stories but to ask for advice on the symposium. She liked the idea.

"What would be a good topic for the nadwa?"

"How about something like women's literature in Syria: problems and ambitions?"

Perfect! Many Arab women writers hate to be identified by gender, not wanting to be considered apart from the men. But since the late 1980s there had been a move in the other direction, with women becoming more self-confident and recognizing the power of the term. In March 1990 in Fez the distinguished Egyptian writer and critic Latifa al-Zayyat had read her stunning testimonial to the second meeting of the Women's Creativity Women's Writing group. In it she reflected on her past rejection of the term "women's literature"; it was a form of self-defense because critics had trivialized literature produced by women in order to exclude it from the literary heritage. Since the 1960s she had refused this categorization. Now, however, things had changed: "Equality between men and women also means acknowledging difference and that difference does not necessarily mean that one is better than the other [only that one should take] into consideration the social and historical conditions in which the Arab woman is raised" (2004, 413–415). Echoes of the speech had resounded around the Arab world. Some adopted the message of the manifesto; others rejected it as the ravings of an old woman. I wanted to know what Syrian women thought.

When Casper first suggested the nadwa, I worried that the American Cultural Center was not the right site. But she insisted that we stick with it. That way we needn't worry about getting a permit. Public events not organized by an official government or Baath Party group but on Syrian soil need a permit from an appropriate ministry. Diplomatic missions are considered to be on their own soil, even in the heart of the Syrian capital and a stone's throw from an Asad palace.

There is a long precedent for cultural events, especially edgy ones, to be held in foreign cultural centers. In 1969 the highly politicized Thorn Theater staged its first show in the Soviet Cultural Center in Damascus. The foreign venue frees the organizers from bureaucratic arbitrariness. I knew how arbitrary ministerial approval could be. Two weeks earlier a lecture tour I had been asked to give at the four universities of Damascus, Homs, Aleppo, and Latakia was "postponed." Two days before it was due to start, Saliha Sunqur, the minister of higher education since 1993, had invited me to her offices. After listening politely for a few minutes, she regretted the inappropriateness of my topic, "Women and War." How could I talk about war when everyone was talking peace? The timing was bad, she added, since the country was about to celebrate the twenty-second year of its victory over Israel (the 1973 Tishrin War) as well as its silver jubilee of the Corrective Movement. She dismissed my proposal to change the title to "Women and Peace." She, too, was a writer and she knew as well as I did how important titles are. They can't be changed just like that. I asked if the tour was canceled and she said no, it was not canceled, just postponed.

Casper was right. It was best to stick to one's own space.

"Will anyone be willing to be seen at the American Center?"

"You bet! People love coming to our events. Of course, there are some who will not, or cannot come. Particularly the Foreign Ministry people. But in general there's no problem with the venue."

In fact, several intellectuals were friendly with the officers of the American Center and even of the embassy. Alberto Fernandez, the public affairs officer, was praised for his command of Arabic and also of the contemporary cultural scene. This was not at all what I had expected to be the case in a country so officially anti-American.

Just to be sure, I asked Colette about the American location, and she put my mind at rest. There was no problem with the place, but she insisted that I manage the event carefully.

"Your questions should deal with the role of women writers in Syrian society today. Who's coming?"

"I've already spoken with Houda Naamani. She's excited at the thought of coming home."

"Why Houda?"

"I thought it would be interesting to include someone who writes from abroad."

"Beirut's not abroad," Colette snapped.

I decided not to pursue the point. Ever since the Syrian invasion into Lebanon in 1976, there had been tension over the relationship between these two countries that European powers had divided into two separate nation-states and then placed under the French Mandate. The Lebanese resented the Syrian incursion, and many Syrians felt that their almost twenty years' presence in Lebanon confirmed that it was part of Syria, greater Syria that is.

"What about some young women?" I asked. "I've not yet met any. What are their concerns? Whom should we invite?"

"Young people aren't writing. You have to understand that ever since the *khaiba* [disappointment] of 1989, no new voices have been heard because no one has the heart to write."

"Why not?"

"You cannot imagine what 1989 did to our young people. They lost their moorings. They had been brought up to believe that socialism was the only moral good and then, overnight, the system imploded. They had to find guidance from somewhere else. It's still too early to know what they are going to do and whether they will be able to write and create at all."

Three years later, while I was teaching in the University of Bucharest, I heard the same characterization of the collapse of the Soviet Union. Those who had lived through the hard days of the cold war could not imagine how a new wave of literature could come out of such "disappointment." Ancien regimists were very pessimistic. Although I was not convinced that there were no young writers, I gave up on the younger generation's participation since I was coming up against a brick wall.

"Really, you know," Colette added, "you should invite Ulfat Idilbi."

chapter three

NO SUCH THING AS

WOMEN'S LITERATURE

A few days later I was trudging up Mount Qasyun to Muhajireen, the gentrified neighborhood where Ulfat Idilbi lived. This lovely mountain looming up over Damascus has inspired poets and painters over the centuries, yet its reality is less romantic than its view from afar. Originally, Mount Qasyun was not considered habitable, but it did shelter fugitives of all sorts. Hence the name Muhajireen, or migrants, given to one of the lower tiers of the slopes. With time, the illegal migrants would set up amenities, make the area home, and

then the city moved in and turned no-man's land into a new neighborhood, with a name, running water, and sewers; then, of course,
the government imposed taxes. Tier after tier of Mount Qasyun had
been tamed and urbanized. At the bottom lived the wealthy and the
middle classes, and near the top, an area that was not yet acknowledged by the municipality of Damascus and therefore not subject to
taxes or city services, was the latest wave of immigrants, Lebanese
who had escaped from the civil war and its aftermath. In other words,
the higher you climb, the more squalid the conditions.

Ulfat Idilbi

Ulfat Idilbi lived near the bottom of Mount Qasyun, in the fashionable area. I arrived a little early, not knowing how long it would take
to get to her place. But she was ready. At seventy-eight, she was an
elegant woman comfortable on her stiletto heels. She ushered me
into an exquisite room with a commanding view of Damascus from
its huge picture windows. The salon was bright with the light of the
sun that bathed furniture inlaid with mother-of-pearl and chairs and
settees covered in pale Damask silk. The intricate pattern of the Isfa-
han carpet was visible through the glass-topped coffee table, with its
silver bowls of pistachio nuts and sugarcoated almonds.

Ulfat Idilbi is considered the grande dame of Syrian literature
and women's culture. In 1954, she published her first collection of
short stories, *Damascene Stories*. They speak about Salhiya, the old
district of Damascus, where she had been brought up but which even
then was being torn down. Her stories memorialize a lost past when
women were strong. She wanted women to know their own strengths
and weaknesses, rather than blaming men without understanding
why they act the way they do. Unlike Colette al-Khuri's early work
that focused on women's psychological and physical needs, Idilbi's
stories present young men who do not understand women, and because they are naïve, confused, and indoctrinated, these men are
unhappy. Her focus during the 1950s on strong women and their
impact on men gradually faded. Her simple stories begin to reflect

wryly on how some women cope and score short-lived victories and how others embrace an exploitive system to eke out whatever benefit they can.

Then in 1980, she published *Damascus Smile of Sadness*, a well-received novel about a woman whose strength and intelligence cannot overcome the oppressiveness of her milieu. Sabriya gives up her lover, a revolutionary who was killed in action, to devote herself to her selfish father until his death in 1947, a day after the *jala'*, the expulsion of the French. She is now completely alone, and although he had abused her the most she is the only one to want to honor her father. Her brothers resent the money she spends on a whirling dervish ceremony, and they fret about what to do with her. She summons her niece Salma, and gives her the journal she had kept, exhorting her to read it in order to avoid her aunt's mistakes. Then she hangs herself. In this rewriting of the people's struggle to shake off the French, the fight for freedom consumed the good men, those who sacrificed their loves and lives for the nation, and spared the bad and the stupid. Ulfat was calling for a new future.

Perched on the edge of a chair, teacup daintily held in both hands, Ulfat started to chat. I reminded her of her granddaughter, a successful businesswoman working for Citibank. She showed me photographs. Married at seventeen, Ulfat had been compelled to interrupt her education to raise her family. But she had always written. She was writing during the 1930s when there was virtually no acknowledgment of women's writings, and of course she had not been published outside Syria. By the early 1940s she had enough stories for a collection; she sent them to Mahmud Taymur, the Egyptian pioneer of the Arabic short story.

"I told him that if he thought they were no good I would not write another thing. But Mahmud Taymur responded very favorably. He liked my style and he even offered to write an introduction to the collection. Years later, when the book was about to come out, I decided that I should finally tell Adib al-Taqi Baghdadi, my Arabic teacher who had always pushed me to write. Imagine my disappointment to learn that he had died a month earlier." Wistfully, she added, "So he never knew about *Damascene Stories*."

Unlike Colette al-Khuri, Ulfat had not originally considered herself to be a writer but rather a patron of letters. Always happy in the company of writers and artists, especially women, she decided to regularize such meetings. In 1942 with some women friends she founded the Cultural Association for Women.

"We were so young when we first met in each other's homes. Let me see, I must have been twenty-one. It was Adib Baghdadi again who was instrumental. He encouraged us girls to get together and to read each other's writings. Then, in 1942, we got a permit to set up the association and together we bought an apartment. We had so many projects but they were all designed to promote women's issues. The one I liked best lasted for twenty years. We identified smart girls who could not afford to be educated and we sponsored them through university."

I wondered how these upper-class women found out about talented but underprivileged women whose lives were so different from theirs.

"We worked with school heads. Of course, not all the girls we supported actually earned their degrees. Some married young, like me. We did not penalize them."

Noting my curiosity, Ulfat invited me to attend the next meeting of the association. I accepted with alacrity. Every Tuesday morning at eleven, members met to discuss what was to be done in the coming week. That week it was the turn of Mutia Kilani, the wife of a career ambassador and one of the association's founders, to give a talk about her grandmother, who wrote so much poetry that she ended up working in a study lined with her own manuscripts. Nothing, Mrs. Kilani announced dramatically, remains. When no one commented on this startling statement, I asked what had happened. Some of the women looked uncomfortable. They must have known the story.

"They were burned!"

"Burned?"

My neighbor was getting annoyed, and she whispered in a way designed to end discussion: "Internal revolution." No one told me what that meant.

The meeting looked like a Fellini set. Octogenarians, immaculately dressed, many on spindly high heels, hair dyed pitch black, gathered around a long table in a busy basement to talk about ventures they wanted to support while pretty young women, several veiled, bustled about them. At one point a fifty-year-old photograph of the founders was passed around and Ulfat pointed out to me who had died and which of the survivors was with us in the room, a surprisingly large number. I felt like a witness to the end of an era.

Before the nadwa took place, I went back to Muhajireen a couple of times. Ulfat was a lovely host, always glad to see me and to talk about her writing, but always unwilling to talk about the nadwa.

"I've never participated in an American event."

But, I ventured, wasn't it important for Syrians and Americans to get to know one another? I told her of a meeting I had had with 'Ali al-Qayyim, the deputy minister of culture, and how he had called for building bridges of understanding. I mentioned Colette al-Khuri and Houda Naamani and their enthusiasm for the nadwa.

"Oh, dear! I really don't think I can. I am becoming so forgetful nowadays. I would hate to be there and just forget what I was about to say!" And then she would open one of her books and read out loud as though she were the *hakawati*, the storyteller I had gone to hear at the Nawfara Café behind the Umayyad Mosque, and I the audience. Yet I could not be as good as the Nawfara regulars because they had memorized the entire epic of the folk hero Antar and his lover Abla, and I did not know the plot of her stories.

She wanted me to read *The Story of My Grandfather* (1991). Like Colette al-Khuri she was writing about a male ancestor. Speaking in the voice of her grandmother relating the story of her grandfather to her daughter (Ulfat's mother), she plunges the reader into early nineteenth-century Daghestan in revolt against the Russian imperialists and their vastly superior forces: "Mothers were proud to offer the apples of their eyes for the country" (49). The Ottoman sultan Mahmud in Constantinople betrays Salih, Ulfat's great-great-grandfather, who then takes his eighty-year-old father to Damascus to escape the violence in Daghestan. Thirty-five years after leaving, he returns home to his mother, who is blinded with tears of grief. He pays for her cure and the expenses for her pilgrimage to Mecca.

She stays in Damascus for one year only. Her parting words provide a moral for today's Syrians who have left their country: "Emigration is the Daghestanis' greatest sin" (188).

Ulfat Idilbi's vivid descriptions swept me into this world that in the 1990s was beginning to attract international attention because of renewed resistance to the Russians. I suspected that she was criticizing the Syrians who were leaving rather than standing up to their regime.

Since the mid-1980s, Ulfat had been very active, giving public lectures about the importance of women to Islamic history. She had spoken critically about how Western societies persecuted and continue to persecute creative women like Camille Claudel, the French sculptor.

Before the nadwa I read her most recent essays and stories in *Damascene Breezes* (1990). Angrily anti-Western, they reminded me of al-Khuri's October War stories. In light of what I read, I was surprised that she had even agreed to meet with me. At the last moment, she called to say that she was so worried about one of her sons whose cancer had returned that she could not do anything.

"Last time they told me only when he had completed the treatment. But this time they're telling me when he's still sick. I don't know what to believe. I'm afraid he's dead." Silence, and then I heard quiet sobs. She was not talking to me but rather rehearsing her anguish on the phone. I did not know what to say. He died a few months later.

Salons and Mallahat al-Khani

During the weeks leading up to the nadwa, I kept checking with Colette al-Khuri. She seemed a perfect weathervane for the evening. As a member of Parliament she provided the event with political legitimacy, and as a pioneer of feminist outspokenness she would give others license to speak out openly. We agreed on the kinds of questions I should pose. She liked the topics and urged me to invite women of different political and religious persuasions.

"The nadwa panelists should not represent the old right only."

So I went out in search of the left, even if it was not so new. I came up with Mallahat al-Khani (1935–2003) and Nadia Khust (b. 1935), and Colette approved because they were both communists, or had been.

I met Mallahat al-Khani at the salon of Hanan Nijmi, a lawyer. Syria has a tradition of women hosting gatherings of intellectuals. Already in the late nineteenth century, the poet and journalist Marianna Marrash (1849–1919) was bringing together writers and artists in her home in Aleppo. The luminaries of the day recited poetry and discussed literature in a lively atmosphere animated by Marianna's piano and the guests' lutes and oboes. In 1922, Mary Ajami founded the Women's Literary Club. In 1942, the year Ulfat founded the Cultural Association for Women, Zahra al-'Abid, wife of Prime Minister Muhammad 'Ali al-'Abid, launched Zahra's Circle. It was the first salon in Syria to bring men and women together in a public space. Ulfat told me that it was at this salon that she first appeared in public unveiled. Nadia Khust was the most recent addition to salon conveners. In 1992 she launched Arabesques, a salon that she held in an art gallery. Although a communist, she saw no paradox in her presiding over a "bourgeois" salon, and she used the word without apology when we met. Arabesques met irregularly and infrequently.

Hanan Nijmi's salon, however, was regular and frequent. Every first Thursday of the month since 1979, Hanan had hosted local intellectuals and international visitors in her downtown Hamra apartment attached to her legal office. During my six months in Damascus, she hosted evenings as diverse as a postmortem on the 1995 international meeting of women in Beijing, a reading of a new story by Mallahat al-Khani, and a lecture on secularism by the philosopher Ahmad Barqawi.

At 6 P.M., people started to show up. That was the drill. Guests mill around for half an hour; they drink juice and eat canapés and catch up on the past month. At 6:30 the presentation is made and discussion lasts until 9:30. Then the meeting breaks down into informal groups that may stay until after midnight. I asked Hanan whether 'Isa al-Fattuh was right to suggest that the salons of French women like Madame de Staël had influenced Arab women who had hosted salons for the past one hundred years (al-Fattuh 1994, 80–93).

"Good heavens, no! This is Damascus through and through! We have a tradition of *ziyarat* [visits]. Once a month or so people get together for the evening. The only difference here is that my salon is specifically cultural. It is not literary only. Journalists, psychiatrists, and university professors often attend. Of course, many writers come."

I was being reprimanded for a faux pas. How could I liken something in Syria to something from somewhere else?

"Have you met Ahmad Barqawi? He teaches philosophy at Damascus University."

"No, I've not yet had the pleasure, but I did hear your speech 'Consciousness of Freedom' during the Asad Book Fair in September." I wanted to ask him how he had dared to be so outspoken. How could he even think of saying "I rebel therefore I am"? However, when I started to frame the questions, I noticed him pull back a bit. I stammered something about liking his lecture, embarrassed that I apparently had committed an indiscretion. In Damascus of the mid-1990s at least, politically daring statements could be made in many different ways so long as the veil of abstraction or allegory remained firmly in place.

"Gosh, it's almost time for the presentation! Maybe we should sit down."

At 6:30 sharp Hamida 'Ali Man started to talk about her experience in Beijing, where the international UN conference for women had taken place a month earlier. Syria had sent thirteen women and Lebanon 138. Hamida rolled her eyes when she laid out the different agendas that women from the global North and South had presented. She denounced Western feminists for their obsession with sexual orientation and their disinterest in Asian and African women's calls for equality of opportunity. At this point, the audience intervened. They were a bit dubious about this binarized characterization of the conference. A veiled woman and a man dominated the discussion. She insisted on the importance of giving women their rights in order to strengthen society, while he waxed lyrical about the rights women already enjoy in Muslim societies, especially in Syria. The women gave each other knowing looks. Hanan interrupted.

"You're both right and you're both wrong. We have to pay attention to the enormous diversity of women's situations, especially here. How can we generalize even only about Syrian women when we know how far apart our worlds are. On the one hand, we have the peasant woman from the Jazira [the northeastern region of Syria, where the majority of the population are Kurds] who works all day while her husband hangs around like Antar."

Everyone laughed at the image of a local farmer giving himself the airs of a folk hero.

"And then we have Madame X in Abu Rummana at home all day waiting for her husband to take her out dressed up like a doll. She has become *sul'a*, a commodity, who must submit to his every wish and need. She has absolutely no freedom. What, I wonder, does Madame X have in common with Antar's wife?"

Again, people laughed. Hanan had a nice, light way about her and years of practice had taught her how to be diplomatic while managing an argument that was veering toward the explosive, or even only the overly polemical. Hanan 's salon was not the place for grandstanding.

The rest of the evening was spent meeting people. It was then that I met Mallahat al-Khani. She told me that at the next salon she would be reading from one of her latest stories. She hoped I'd come.

Mallahat was a warm, feisty woman and very direct. She was thrilled to be invited to the nadwa (nothing like striking while the iron is hot) and she wanted to make sure that I had read some of her writings beforehand. I looked for her books in the Damascus bookstores, of which there are not very many, but came up empty-handed. Local bookstores were not interested in local authors. Mallahat lent me her novel *The Horseless Carriage* (1981) and *A Multicolored Woman* (1987), a collection of stories about relationships between men and women that focus on a crisis point that has been brewing for a while (see Midfai 1996). Her heroines claim the right to work so that they may enjoy personal fulfillment and economic independence that enhance the well-being of the family.

Later she invited me to meet some of her friends. The women were chatty and friendly, with the exception of Mayya al-Rahbi, a writer and medical doctor, who was quite cold and, like Barqawi, very suspicious. Why was an American interested in Syrian literature? Why women? Mallahat teased her that I wasn't a spy. That calmed things down a bit and the conversation moved elsewhere. They all had a good laugh when they heard that my husband, Bruce, and I were living in the apartment of a retired general who kept asking us why we did not tune in to Israeli TV stations. Oh, yes, they knew him well! Dr. Mayya, however, was still peeved.

"Had Mallahat not invited me today, you would never have heard of me. You would not have read anything that I wrote."

"That's why I am staying for several months, because it's so hard to know what's going on in the Syrian literary world."

Somewhat mollified, Dr. Mayya then echoed what Nadia al-Ghazzi had said at the beginning of my stay: "Yes, I know. Our literature is not known abroad."

She suggested that I read her latest collection that happened to be on sale in the bookstore opposite the Cham Palace Hotel in the middle of modern Damascus.

The title story of *A Liberated Woman for Sale* (Rahbi 1995) tells how the wife of a "feminist" discovers that her husband is a misogynist tyrant for whom women are servants or prostitutes. Like other Arab women writers, Mayya al-Rahbi insists that the radical armchair theorist must take responsibility for the activism that gives his discourse meaning. "Al-bahlul" (The fool) was an openly political story about a foolish young man who accepts all humiliations—he even obeys the director's youngest child's command to pull down his pants—while yelling at his own subordinates. Since al-Rahbi had explicitly asked me to read this story, I thought that a measure of trust had been established between us. Perhaps she had overcome her distaste for Americans. Might she be willing to participate in the nadwa? When I asked her, she recoiled in horror.

Nadia Khust and the Nadwa

It was time to confirm who would participate in the nadwa and I had not yet asked Nadia Khust. She was more politically engaged than any of the women I had met. In the fraught year of 1967, she published at her own expense a collection of sentimental short stories about women's patriotism under the title *I Love Damascus*. During the summer of 1994, Nadia had led the charge against Adonis, the Syrian poet in exile between Beirut and Paris, who had called for dialogue between Arab and Israeli intellectuals as part of normalization.

The Oslo Accords were less than a year old, and a few intellectuals had felt that it was time to declare some kind of truce with Israel. For over thirty years Israel had been Syria's constant enemy. It was Israel that shaped Syrian identity; to be Syrian was to be at war with Israel. The 1982 invasion of Lebanon fanned the flames of enmity for a while. The Gulf War nine years later polarized the Arab world between Saddam Hussein's Iraq and Iraqi-occupied Kuwait and Kuwait's pro-Israeli U.S.-led saviors. To the surprise of many, Syria sided with Kuwait against its Baath rival in Iraq: "The enemy of my enemy is my friend." A breach had been opened in the hard-line position Syria had been proud to present to Israel and to the world.

Three years later Adonis declared himself for dialogue with Israeli counterparts. Syrian intellectuals had to adjudicate between two official positions: long-time opposition to Israel and a new openness to the West. Nobody seemed to know what the safe position was. The Arab Writers Union, after debating the issue, came down against Adonis and expelled him. After his expulsion several writers, including the playwright Saadallah Wannus (1941–1997), resigned in protest. Confusion reigned.

Nadia Khust might be termed an urban activist. For years she has protested the incursion of real estate developers into Suq Saruja, the neighborhood that she claims is disappearing under the spreading concrete of the modern city. The remains of her childhood home, she told me, lay somewhere beneath Shari 'al-Thawra, or Revolution Street, the huge thoroughfare that cuts through Damascus. In conversation with anthropologist Christa Salamandra, Khust said, "The most beautiful houses in Damascus—their decorations, trees, fountains, and sitting rooms—all ended up under Revolution Street, severely limiting the number of historic buildings along the hajj route (the caravan route of the Muslim Pilgrimage to Mecca)" (Salamandra

2004, 78; also see 139–140). I was struck by the similarity with the massive Casa Populorui that Ceausescu built in the 1980s over the crushed homes of thousands of Romanians.

Nadia is not afraid to point the finger of blame at those she suspects of being responsible for what she openly terms a "crime." She was not afraid to publish books on the subject. *Departure from Paradise* (1989), *No Room for the Stranger* (1990), and *Damascus, Memory of People and Stones* (1993) can be read as elegies to the world she was watching disappear.[1]

One evening Nadia took me through Suq Saruja to show me how the old city was being destroyed. Taking a flashlight out of her purse she shone its light on a crumbling wall. Then she told me to look closely. Upon inspection it turned out that the wall was not spontaneously falling apart. It was being systematically scraped and chiseled till it started to give and finally collapse.

Nadia was leading a multipronged campaign to expose those involved in the "crime." She convinced city counselors to take some of her complaints seriously. She was proud of her success in saving the Madrasa Tarikhiya, a religious school founded in the twelfth century by Sitt al-Sham, a sister of Saladin. It was there that she gave a talk the municipality had asked her to deliver on the destruction of the old city. Dignitaries were invited, and so the municipality had to clean and restore the place.

Nor was she afraid to publish her positions. The title story of *No Room for the Stranger* is a ringing indictment of the government. A man complains to the Historical Association that a certain Yusuf, a national hero, is haunting his house. Without even asking him where he lived the people in the association "looked at him approvingly while he burnt incense to chase away the specters and they signed a demolition permit and then a building permit to construct a place with big windows and balconies that would keep ghosts out" (Khust 1990, 18). Documents were then gathered and piled high on a cart pulled by four mules "confirming that History never passed through that neighborhood. And even the mules looked angry" (18). The hero who died for his country is thus erased from History. The director's assistant is particularly proud of the deal, crowing that whereas directors come and go, he is always there. Rumor has it that he "could disappear heroes and events without anyone noticing, [for History remains] mute when we do not utter it" (21). When Yusuf returns from the dead to protest, the director and his assistant collude in hiding the evidence. No proof, however compelling, can persuade those who are determined to erase people and events from the pages of the history books. No one and nothing should interfere in their prospering from real estate speculation. In 1995, Khust published *Love in Syria*, a huge novel on the lost world of Suq Saruja.

The night of the nadwa, 22 October 1995, only Mallahat al-Khani and Houda Naamani turned up on time. Mallahat walked around the hall greeting people she knew. Huda had come from Beirut the night before. She spent the afternoon hanging a few of her abstract canvases that she had brought for an exhibition at the American Center. The room was crowded but only two of the speakers had turned up. How embarrassing! At 6:01 Colette made a dramatic appearance. She swept up the stairs in a black taffeta ball gown and surrounded by a cortege of old men and beautiful young women. Nadia came a quarter of an hour later.

I immediately launched into my introduction: "Welcome to this special event, during which we shall celebrate the literary achievements of Syrian women writers. Today's symposium will look into the situation for women writers here in Syria and in neighboring Lebanon."

At this point, the loudspeaker system broke down.

"Women have long been active in Syrian cultural production," I shouted. "Although we have little information from the nineteenth century, the intensity of women's cultural activity during the past seventy years suggests that twentieth-century women intellectuals in Syria did not emerge out of a void."

"We can't hear a word!"

I walked into the middle of the crowd and, carrying my heavy notebook—an ugly beast I had thought no one would see on the podium—I started to read as though out of the Gospels on a Sunday morning in Hillsborough, North Carolina. Actually, it was not such a bad thing: the failure of technology in the American Center loosened and cheered up everyone. Another bonus was that we had the audience's rapt, if strained, attention. What was not so great was that the panelists had to jump up and down and scream to make themselves heard, sometimes separately but sometimes, alas, together.

"There are many women writing in Syria today," I continued. "Over the past decade women's voices everywhere in the Arab world have become louder. In previously colonized societies women were the first to engage the crisis of colonial legacies at their deepest level, where personal roles and relationships are distorted. They write to stimulate readers to reflect on their own political situations."

More shouts from the back made me realize that I would have to abandon the historical framing and just get on with the show.

"I would like to begin with Ulfat Idilbi's 1986 lecture, titled 'Women and Genius' in *Damascene Breezes*, that reminds us that women poets were numerous in the pre-Islamic and early Islamic periods, but all that has reached us is the elegy, women mourning the loss of their men. Do you believe that women in the past wrote elegies only? Does the creative woman face fewer obstacles today than she has traditionally? Colette, was Ulfat right to say that were Camille Claudel alive today, she would not suffer as she did a hundred years ago?"

"Before answering the question I have to address a major issue. Can we really say that there is such a thing as 'women's literature'? Isn't there just literature that happens to be written by men or by women?"

Each panelist confirmed that there was no such thing as women's literature, that to say that there was meant that it might be inferior to men's literature.[2] But they did talk about what it meant to be a woman writer, about the particular problems women face balancing responsibilities of home and creativity, and how those problems affect what they write.

"Women writers sometimes have to stop writing altogether," Mallahat said, "so that their literary preoccupations should not interfere in their domestic duties. I had to stop for ten years while my kids were growing up."

She even quoted Latifa al-Zayyat to describe "women's literature" as highly personal. Nodding, Nadia added, "Women's writing has a special *nakha*, a particular smell. Domestic experiences give writing extra perspective and depth."

She provided me with an opening: "Doesn't this mean that there's a difference between men's and women's writings that is not, of course, essential but rather experiential?"

An audience member stood up and suggested that my obsession with women's literature was an American hang-up.

Nadia elaborated on the special problems confronting women writers who try to balance family needs and professional pulls without support from the government. Colette contradicted her: "Any obstacles women writers face come from unsupportive men and not because there are any institutional blocks."

"For whom are you writing?" I went on to my next question. "Has your readership changed over time?"

Colette stood up dramatically and, throwing her hands in the air, she declaimed, "Writing is a way of screaming with my fingers. I have always written for everyone, because I want as large a readership as possible. How else could I compete with television and newspapers?"

The audience laughed.

Mallahat spoke next: "I think I have always written for people like me. I try to uncover the truth so that those who are similarly situated can look to my stories for help because they have recognized themselves in my heroines."

Houda seemed tentative, as she had been throughout the evening. She was apprehensive about the welcome she would receive after having been gone so long: "I struggle to communicate and to be clear, but people find my poetry difficult. That's why I paint. It is more direct." She went on to say how happy she was to be back in her native Damascus.

Her comment allowed me to ask the panelists what they thought about writing at home and abroad. Spontaneously, Mallahat said that there was no difference for her because she did not have to leave Syria to feel a stranger. Internal and external exile felt the same. For Nadia leaving Damascus gave her distance to look at her life and her country. Houda, whose presence had made the question salient, said that her poetry had never ceased to be inspired by love for her native Damascus. She had checked with me beforehand about the question of exile and I reassured her that I had spoken to Colette and was pretty confident that this was the right way to address the issue. But I was wrong. Perhaps the American venue changed Colette's mind about the suitability of much of what we had discussed beforehand.

"How can you say that Beirut is *ghurba* [exile]? It's not outside Syria. The Lebanese and the Syrians are one people!"

This political jibe provoked muted titters. Nadia picked up the slack.

"Whether I write here or abroad my main aim is to get through to the next generation, and I hope that they understand what I mean."

Nadia had provided me with a perfect segue to my last question, about young women writers.

"My last question comes from Marie Seurat and Ulfat Idilbi, who both were optimistic that their daughters, real and fictive, could learn from their mistakes. In her autobiography, Marie hopes that her daughters would one day 'find the best part of my revolt, that they will not let themselves be slaughtered, *mater*, this atrocious word that I heard when I was a child, that they might become provocative, wild artists, that they enrich themselves from several societies so that no one will curb them or shape them into something they are not' [Seurat 1988, 241]. In Idilbi's *Damascus, Smile of Sadness* Sabriya, before committing suicide, gives her niece Salma the journal she has kept throughout the years she suffered in her father's house. This gift comes as a gesture of adoption between the childless woman and her chosen heir. Who is your Salma?"

My question was longer than the answers and no one talked about young women writers. The starting had finally exhausted us.

Later that evening I was cornered and questioned. The "nonexistent" young generation was angry that I had not tried harder to locate them. They might have expected that it would turn out like that! Colette Banha had just published *The First Confession* (1995), a collection of short stories primarily about divorce and science fiction. What, she wanted to know, had happened to the dialogue that had been promised between them and these established writers? It was the first time I had heard about such a promise.

"It's always the same!" she complained. "Of course, we're writing feminist fiction. Don't you read the journals *Al-Kifah al-'Arabi* and *Al-Mada*? Had you done so you would not have believed these women when they told you that there was no new talent."

Then, three days later, a member of the Women's Union, a government-sponsored institution like the Arab Writers Union, called to complain to the American Center. Why had she and other union members not been invited to the nadwa? Above all, why had there been no young women writers?

During the past 20 years, Arab regimes have
prevented intellectuals from playing their
leadership roles. They have worked to turn
them into official mouthpieces. Their methods
include oppression and pursuit, confiscation
and prison. . . . There is agreement that the
writer is a witness whose witness must be
silenced . . . so that tyranny can relax
and spread.
—SA'ADALLAH WANNUS,
"The Cultural Program"

chapter four

COMMISSIONED CRITICISM

May came and with it my talk on "Culture Is Humanity's Highest Need" at the French Institute. I gave an overview of women's literary concerns, drawing heavily on the nadwa. Apart from touching lightly on Nadia Khust's urban activism, I did not discuss politics.

Everyone, but especially the chair, seemed tense. Nadia al-Ghazzi was the only woman writer to attend, and she sat in a corner nervously. She was clearly relieved that the talk was almost entirely about women's writings. Not everyone, however, shared her relief that I had not touched on the slogan. During the Q&A someone asked why I had chosen the title "Culture Is Humanity's Highest Need." He had not grasped the connection between the title and the talk.

The following week I had several conversations with people at the Institute. They all criticized the talk, not for the content but for its disconnect from the title. How could I choose a slogan and not take it apart, push it to its limits?

"This phrase frightens us. Don't you see how it hides the instrumentalization of culture? Why did you not talk of censorship? Of newspapers with pages torn out? Why didn't you talk about all those films that are produced and never screened? Or that no one is publishing a word about the present?"

The man in the audience who had been particularly upset confronted me later: "Scholars have a role to play in such a society. You're from the outside. You are protected not only by your country, but also by your universities. You should say how things are! You cannot use a slogan without exposing what it hides. In a *culture aménagée*, where intellectuals risk their freedom for a poem or an article and go to prison [it was the first time I had heard the word in five months of being in the country], it is morally wrong to defend the system."

Referring to a recent article about me published in the official *Baath* newspaper, he said sarcastically that I was free to give nice interviews to newspapers and television. But, he concluded, "you are then complicit with the regime and you are no longer a *chercheur*."

I was an outsider, I risked nothing, and yet I had said nothing. They had thought that I would have the guts to speak out. Clearly they knew what was going on around them, like the socialist Czechs about whom Havel had written: "Individuals need not believe all these mystifications, but they must behave as though they did." Those disappointed in me were saying that although they had to behave as if they believed the mystifications, outsiders should not. I had a moral responsibility to be open and honest and I had shirked it.

When I met with the chair a couple of weeks later, I told him of some of my encounters with his colleagues at the French Institute.

"What did I tell you? You shouldn't have stuck with the title. This is a problem we live every day." He was elliptical as always, leaving the "this" vague. "You merely decorated the subject. You didn't push it. We need vision from the outside. We are very interested to hear what outsiders have to say because they are not involved. So, what is this 'culture' of which the regime speaks? Is it a Syrian culture? Is it specific to this regime? What is the gap between them? Aren't we faced with a situation where the regime is telling us, 'I am more cultured than you, but I will let you produce what you call culture even if I refuse to let it appear in the light of day.' That's how they prevent us from forming a base on which to build. Who knows what the future will bring," he mused. "Because the government sponsors the making of films no one can accuse it of stopping the production of culture. No film is banned. It is just not permitted. You must understand this strange game. The government will never say no. It will just not issue a permit. So: I permit, but someone else has to give you the permit. You move on up the ladder of power and authority trying to get to the one who gives out the actual permit, until you come to a level where there is no longer anyone who issues permits. The purpose of this system is not to produce culture but to *break the Syrian cultural personality*."

Fighting words. He told me about an Assyrian artist from Hasake (capital of the northern province with a Kurdish majority) and member of the Communist Action Party, whose personal papers got lost in the system. When his wife took his case to the top of the bureaucratic ladder, she was told, "We do not give out such papers."

"But they did not refer her to anyone else who could. Look around you when you walk through the streets. Just pay attention." Then in hushed tones: "The danger here is not that people will get sick of what is happening, but that they will forget what it's like to be sick of it. They will become sheep." I thought of Maghut's description of the people's paralyzing fear that "pours out of my pen and my fingers and my eyelashes like milk pouring out of the udder of a sheep returning from the pasture" (2001, 356).

"Look what's happening elsewhere," he concluded. "Go to Romania. See how they treat their gypsies."

In the summer of 1998 I did go to Romania. I learned that the pre-1989 Romanian state also used culture to shape consciousness. In such systems, "discourse has a disproportionately productive role, and especially for one whose self-proclaimed task is to change society, the producers of discourse must be incorporated within the regime" (Verdery 1991, 90–91). Like the Romanians, Syrian intellectuals were producing books, paintings, and films that were entangled in state mechanisms of control. These works did not leave the country; they were absorbed.

Culture after the Fall of the Wall

By the mid-1990s the Syrian state, like socialist Eastern European states before it, was deep into pretending: not to possess an omnipotent and unprincipled police apparatus, to respect human rights, to persecute no one, to fear nothing. Above all, it was pretending to pretend nothing. Colette al-Khuri was right when she told me that 1989 was a critical year in Syria. The collapse of socialism in Eastern Europe compelled a rethinking of the entire ideological framework within which the state had been working since 1970. How could Soviet-style ideologies be adapted to a more capitalistic form of governance? The regime launched into a contradictory project: fashioning a facade of freedom and democracy even while tightening its hold over the public sphere, particularly over cultural production. The Baathist slogan "Unity, Freedom, and Socialism" was touted with a decreased accent on socialism.[1]

Artists and writers had to walk a new, narrower tightrope. Demands for civil liberties were now part of the government's new liberal agenda, yet sometimes such demands were criminalized. How could individuals work with the state while retaining a careful distance from the propaganda machinery? Wedeen writes that many were co-opted: "Individual poets, university professors, artists and playwrights are periodically called upon to help produce the public spectacles and to maintain Asad's cult; the federation of peasants and workers and the professional syndicates of journalists, lawyers, teachers, and doctors, among others are all required at one time or another to conjure up slogans and imagery representing their idealized connection to party and president. Often citizens respond by finding a way to avoid trouble without feeling deeply compromised" (1999, 3).

The sculptor Mustafa ʿAli (b. 1956), an Alawite hippie with enormous talent, provided an unexpected insight into the ways intellectuals negotiated these new, paradoxical conditions while attempting to live in truth. Educated in Syria and Italy, Mustafa was becoming well-known. When I met him in spring 1996 at an American Embassy reception, he was basking in the glow of new national and international attention. He had just completed a huge marble calligraphic sculpture for the Qasr al-Shaʿb, the primary palace of Hafiz Asad overlooking the whole of Damascus. The Ministry of Culture had commissioned him to design and make prizes for the biannual Syrian film festival, and he was beginning to exhibit all over the Arab world.

The government commissions began in the early 1990s. At about that time, he was working on a new series of Giacometti-like bronzes full of hyenas, masks, and cages. The most striking piece was of Imrul Qays, the vagabond poet prince from pre-Islamic Arabia. Mustafa had represented the complicated life of this dissident poet, verses of whose ode every Arab child has to memorize, through a single sculpture. It was a wooden box encasing the poet's head balanced on four long spindly metal legs.

I saw it in his workshop in the Muhyi al-Din Ibn Arabi district. I had come with the artist Hala Faysal, who had also been at the reception. We wandered around the studio and then he took us to the garage now converted into a workshop. It was there that he was working on Imrul Qays. Through the bars at the front of the dark box I could make out the features of a beautiful man. A hyena crouching on top of the box guarded al-malik al-dalil, or the errant king. I had noticed that hyenas figured in several films and novels and I wondered why those wild dogs of the night kept making an appearance.[2]

"What," I asked Mustafa, "does the hyena poised on Imrul Qays's head signify?"

"Death," he responded in a matter-of-fact voice. Hyenas in Arabian lore are thought to deprive humans of speech and motion when they step on their shadow. Hyenas in Syrian cultural production seem to stand in for oppressive authorities that step on people's shadows and silence and freeze them (see Frazer 1976, 251).

"Why did you put this exquisite head in a box? I can hardly see him." Laughing good-naturedly at yet another question, he told me that it was enough that he had given the piece a title. I heard Ghada Samman's reprimand echoing across the fifteen years that separated this evening from the one I had spent with her in war-torn Beirut.

"A work of art should suggest many things. Artists should not place their interpretation between the object and the viewer. Yes, the wood is worm-eaten. That's on purpose."

I had been examining the intricate patterns that worms had woven in the wood. At first I thought that Mustafa had chiseled the marbled designs, but when I looked closer and ran my finger over a perforated piece, I realized they were natural. The box was not designed to withstand the trials of time.

Hala Faysal was at my side during this exchange. The box, she whispered, symbolized repression. It crossed my mind that she must have thought me stupid. On the other hand, this was a rare moment when someone spoke openly about political pressure.

"Do you know why I paint? I paint because writing is too transparent. Art is ambiguous, more difficult to decipher," she went on. Mustafa nodded absentmindedly.

I did not ask Mustafa about the worm-eaten wood, but I noted how carefully he uttered the words "That's on purpose." Was the work designed to implode over a specific period of time? He could gauge the life of the wood based on the rate of the worms' consumption, and so one day the box would just disintegrate, the hyena would fall to the floor, and the vagabond poet prince would finally be free of the cage.

I bought another poet, the third in a series of six bronzes. Skinny, chest thrust forward against the wind, he had ventured to the very edge of a precipice, with one foot poised above the void. Looking straight out into the unknown, but sheltered by a friendly tree, this poet was the incarnation of courage and reckless determination. He was the errant king before the cage and the bars. He was, of course, also Saint-Exupéry's Little Prince on his planet. How did these dissident works jibe with the prizes and the sculptures for the palaces? It seemed incomprehensibly paradoxical unless it was part of the system, a part of what I call commissioned criticism.

"The Poet" by Mustafa ʿAli.

Commissioned Criticism

At its most basic level commissioned criticism is an official and paradoxical project to create a democratic facade. Like licensed criticism, commissioned criticism may be encouraged in times of crisis and tension when "the President no doubt calculates that it is better to have [a] safety valve for popular grievances than to stifle their expression altogether" (*Index on Censorship* 1984, vol. 2, no. 35). The regime gauges how much criticism to release to maintain atomization, acquiescence, and apathy, while curbing any tendency toward insurgency.

The criticism that targets the system but not the leader falls under the category of what Wedeen calls permitted or licensed criticism (1999, 90). When the state permits criticism it is allowing pressure to be released and at the same time it is signaling "to both the regime and to citizens the shifting levels of commitment, obedience, and disobedience, which are otherwise driven underground. Permitted critiques may even help to identify and ferret out disobedient Syrians. . . . The existence of alternative yet carefully circumscribed visions of political life operates as a mechanism of surveillance" (91). The assumption in such theories of licensed criticism is that because everyone knows what is happening, the mystifications are indulged and tolerated. Intellectuals in such a system are always already bought; Moroccans call that kind of critique *intiqad mushtara*, or bought critique. Here Havel's judgment is unequivocal: bought dissidents do not live in truth.

Bought critique is a safety-valve mechanism that allows for what Syrians call *tanaffus*, or breathing. This tanaffus is a moment for sharing unbelief and awareness of injustice; it provides pleasurable release of pent-up pressure. Some have pointed to the double bind of tanaffus. On the one hand, it marks the survival of a collective consciousness of injustice, that I am not alone in my awareness of stifling oppression and moral betrayal. On the other hand, the anxious reader or spectator can breathe deeply for a moment and then return to life as it was without thinking about changing it. This is the danger of tanaffus: it allows injustice to persist. In the 1970s Sa'adallah Wannus warned against the drugging effect of tanaffus in the dramatic arts because it invites spectators to "deposit their burdens on their chairs before leaving the theater." Such tanaffus makes the intolerable tolerable (1996, 36–37). The urban activist publications of Nadia Khust and the writings of Muhammad Maghut belong to tanaffus literature. Neither takes on the leadership, but only the state and its employees. Consider this poem by Maghut:

> Whenever I glimpse an official paper on the threshold
> Or a helmet from a crack in the door,
> My bones rattle,
> Tears race, and my terrified blood
> Jolts in all directions
> As if an eternal legion of police
> Chased it from vein to vein. (quoted in Kahf 2001, 233)

As was the case with his *I Shall Betray My Homeland*, Maghut could write what he liked with apparent impunity because he did not touch the leader. He concentrated instead on the flaws in all governments that deceive their people and on the people who tolerate this treatment and live in a swamp of fear. He did not propose any kind of action. This is therapeutic, tanaffus writing that allows readers to feel better because they are not alone.

Commissioned criticism, however, is different from licensed criticism. Situated at the nexus of the permitted and the transgressive, it is the mechanism that exploits what is ambiguous in Syrian arts of domination. It is not merely the toleration of transgressive practices that bridge the cognitive gap between the lies of government pronouncements and the reality of everyday life. Rather, it is the regime's Machiavellian manipulation of dissidence. The state pressures dissidents to continue their dissident practice. It is precisely because they are dissident that they matter. The state then tries to coopt the criticism. Commissioned criticism is a state-sponsored practice that performs official accountability for the rosy rhetoric of slogans while attempting to convert real dissident practice into state ideology.

How does commissioned criticism work? The regime sends mixed signals to those who are veering toward dissidence: You are being

watched, you are pushing at the limits, you may be risking your freedom and even your life, yet you must continue to push at the limits
and we will publicize your critiques. Intellectuals are made to understand that they have the responsibility to critique and that the refusal
to do so may be no less risky than its excessive deployment. Under
such circumstances, dissidents do not know whether what they write
or paint or scupt or turn into moving images corresponds to an inner
drive or is part of a disguised Mephistophelean pact. They must
always ask themselves whether or not their courage is authorized.
Does it serve those it targets? Who is licensed and who is not? Who
will end up rich and who in jail? Such criticism helped the state fashion the facade of freedom, democracy, and civil society while trying
to morph political dissidents into docile bodies.

Commissioned criticism is a process, a disciplinary mechanism
that controls the public square by keeping the conditions of cultural
production uncertain and unpredictable but always connected with
the government. It enables what Michel Foucault called the production of docile bodies by means of "a policy of coercions that act upon
the body. . . . This discipline produced subjected and practiced bodies,
docile bodies. . . . The order does not need to be explained or formu-
lated; it must trigger off the required behavior and that is enough. . . .
It is a question not of understanding the injunction but of perceiving
the signal and reacting to it immediately, according to a more or less
artificial code. . . . It is a technique of training, of *dressage*" (1991, 138,
166). Contradictory orders and arbitrary rewards ensure slavish obedience.

Criticism might be commissioned in any cultural form. The Ministry of Culture published socially and politically sensitive books, like
Ghassan al-Jaba'i's *Banana Fingers* (see chapter 7), but it would not distribute them on the open market; they were sent to remote regional
cultural centers or Arab book fairs, where they fashioned for foreign
consumption the facade of Syrian democracy and civil rights. The
National Film Organization, under the Ministry of Culture, had an
absolute monopoly on film production. It commissioned, approved,
and funded the making of two or three films annually. These films
were sometimes very explicit. In Usama Muhammad's *Stars During*

the Day the main character is a man on the make who comes from the Alawite region in the north. People were quick to point out how like the president the main actor looked. Even the house in which the action takes place looks exactly the same as the house in which Hafiz Asad was born (see Seale 1989, 278). The hero keeps telling his extended family how much he loves them while stealing whatever they have of value. The Israeli soldier at the front is more sympathetic, more human than the paterfamilias when he asks a Syrian soldier whether it is not time for him to take a break and go home. The film was not banned, it was just not released. Films were the property of the government that could do with them what it wanted. It was the state that decided when, where, and whether to show a Syrian film (see chapter 6).[3] The Ministry of Culture monitored the theater from original concept to script to rehearsal to performance. A play might jump all the hurdles only to be canceled after opening night because a meaning hidden in the written words would jump right out when uttered by an intelligent actor to an intelligent audience.

Reception seems to have been calibrated to determine sanctions for a sliding scale of criticism that in turn determined the extent of distribution. The least available genre, theater, was the most radical. A dramatic performance that is not recorded disappears with no trace beyond its memory in the mind of the spectator. The next level of availability was books and films. They, too, might be highly critical and daring because even though they were available to be reread and reviewed the government could more or less ensure their disappearance. Television and the newspapers, on the other hand, with their large audiences were more circumspect (Lobmeyer 1994, 81). The papers might "be encouraged to write about the housing crisis, the lack of adequate street cleaning, or occasionally even such issues as failures of the state sector, official corruption, or the sins of the new bourgeoisie. After the regime allows discussion of such matters, it often then decides that things have gone far enough and again closes this small opening" (HRW 1991, 116). Television was the least critical medium until the arrival of satellite television. Syrian soap operas written for Ramadan audiences tended to tackle current problems, especially corruption (Peterson 1977). The many festivals and exhibitions projected on state television created the impression that there were many venues for private persons to come together to form a public. Yet the coverage betrayed itself, since there were no spontaneous diffusions. The reporter would recite a familiar script while officials' mouths moved in the background. People would be shown talking to reporters, but the voice-over of the official script was all the audience heard.

Syrians understood that critical discourse existed and that it might well be government-instigated. In fact, they had a term for intellectuals they believed had let themselves be manipulated: *muharrij*, or court jester. This jester was a figure of fun, worse than the apparatchik, who at least did not pretend to be what he was not. The problem with the word was how freely it was bandied about. Writers who were members of the Arab Writers Union, like the late Mamduh 'Adwan, were especially likely to be so labeled because they were seen to be in the pay of the state. The Writers Union provided social goods like housing and health care that would otherwise be prohibitively expensive. Those who produced trenchant criticisms of the regime or its leader without immediate retribution were suspected of being supported, of being *min 'azmat al-raqaba* (literally, "a bone in the neck," meaning to be tied to the state), of being court jesters. How else, people wondered, could they be so outspoken? And so to be Alawite, to live in an Arab Writers Union apartment, and to be critical with impunity were automatically suspect.

The stigma of being a court jester was hard to overcome and it became an easy way to harm a rival. In 1978 'Adwan, author of seventeen collections of poetry and twenty-seven plays, complained of the agonizing situation of intellectuals who have to choose "between daily security and accepting one's own debasement, on the one hand, and revolting on the other hand, and in so doing risking one's life. Between these two possibilities there's a thread, an operating margin, fine as a hair, which consists in doing something without committing suicide but playing instead in the best way with the bureaucratic contradictions of the regime, exercising artistic sharpness" (quoted in Gaston 1978, 25–35). In other words, intellectuals had to negotiate between twin evils: state control and attempts at cooptation on the one hand, and perceptions of appropriation on the other hand. Between this Scylla and that Charybdis they had to find an effective way to articulate dissent.

The Fantasy of Choice

Slavoj Žižek insists that however preposterous the power discourse and however unbelievable the slogans, intellectuals must take official rhetoric seriously: "Insofar as power relies on its 'inherent transgression,' then—sometimes at least—*over-identifying* with the explicit power discourse—*ignoring* this inherent obscene underside and simply taking the power discourse at its (public) word, acting as if it really means what it explicitly says (and promises)—can be the most effective way of disturbing its smooth functioning" (2000, 220). In a context where culture and freedom are the regime's favorite words, intellectuals should take the official language at its word and act *as if.* But Žižek's as if is different from Havel's; it is prescriptive and not descriptive. He is telling citizens of authoritarian states how to behave, rather than analyzing their actual behavior. Žižek's as if did not mean people were acting as if they believed the unbelievable; to the contrary, it meant acting as if the regime really meant what it explicitly said and promised. This is what the philosopher Ahmad Barqawi did when he talked about freedom in the Asad Library in September 1995. This is what Syrian dissidents were doing in the mid-1990s when they behaved as if slogans like "Freedom, Unity, Socialism" and "Culture Is Humanity's Highest Need" meant what they said and promised.

How can intellectuals deal with the regime's mystifications, particularly its projection of the fantasy of choice? For Žižek, the fantasy underlying the facade of democracy is enabled by empty symbolic gestures that produce the illusion that there is a choice when all know there is none. Confronted with such a choice and knowing that one cannot choose not to choose, the survivor must know how to choose. The only way to undo such a system, in Žižek's view, is to take the power discourse at its word, to pretend the choice is real. Above all, dissidents must learn how to function within the logic of the ideology which "is a systematically distorted communication: a text in which, under the influence of unavowed social interests (of domination, etc.), a gap separates its 'official,' public meaning from its actual intention—that is to say, in which we are dealing with an unreflected tension between the explicit enunciated content of the text and its pragmatic presuppositions" (1994, 10). The gap yawning between the fantasy of choice and the reality of its absence is where dissidents should insert their demands and challenges.

In 1970 the playwright Sa'adallah Wannus proposed a theater that would bridge this gap between official promises and their empty reality. In *Al-Maarifa* (1970, vol. 104) he wrote about a new Arab theater that would explode the cognitive dissonance between sound, meaning, and intention. The interplay between the words of the actors, their gestures, and the intelligent audience creates an organic relationship between the dissident playwright, the director, the actor, and the spectators. Whereas the written critique may pass the censor, the performance might not. The silences, the hidden innuendoes come to light when an actor's wink makes the audience complicit with the deeper meaning of the words. In a later interview Wannus elaborated what he meant. Like Barqawi and Maghut, he was working with the mystifications surrounding the word *freedom*: it may look harmless on paper, but it sounds dangerous when articulated in a particular tone of voice (Wannus 1996, 31).

Drama, like film, is created for an audience, a group of people who share the experience merely by being together in a theater. They do not have to do anything; they do not have to say anything to anyone to be bonded to those others in that hall who have understood what they have understood. The audience continually shapes the play. The production must remain supple enough to react to its reception; it must never rigidify. It should not have the palliative effect of tanaffus theater that makes the intolerable tolerable. Rather, it should disturb and spur spectators to act to change their situation (Wannus 1996, 34–37). Wannus wanted his audience to be alert to hints and gestures and to resist every attempt to drug the senses. They "must never forget that what is happening in front of them affects them. . . . It is they who are responsible for the performance" (38–39). They must work with the dramaturge, the director, and the actors to expose the mystifications of the official ideology.

For Wannus nice words like *freedom* and *progress* should compel attention to the ways these words affect us "as individuals with our desires and urgent needs for freedom, as also our ability to say 'I' without shame. . . . This national program can only succeed and become a reality when this 'I' opens up and practices its freedom and expresses itself without shame, pretense or dread" (quoted in Ilyas 1996, 104). Like Ahmad Barqawi, Wannus directly implicated the regime, asking how a constitution based on freedom prevents individuals from practicing this freedom without shame, pretense, or dread. Both were reading the ideology literally, pretending the fantasy was not a lie, and then acting within its logic. They wrote what their conscience compelled even when they knew that they risked their freedom and sometimes their lives. They opted to live in truth even without knowing what difference they could make in an environment where the artistic gesture felt futile at best and an act of collaboration with the state at worst.

I read their daring as a challenge to Walter Benjamin's pessimistic account of art in the age of mechanical reproduction. He feared that the new and inevitable imbrication of art with politics opened it up to unprecedented uses. Aestheticized politics was the badge of fascism, politicized art the hallmark of communism. However, when Benjamin lamented the loss of the aura, predicated on the work's authenticity and uniqueness in time and place, he left out the contestatory practice of dissident artists. He overlooked the moral authority invested in oppositional artists, writers, and filmmakers. His theory did not address the impact of a story, a piece of sculpture, or a film in which readers recognize their own anguished situations. The electric charge at the moment of recognition and the appreciation for the artist's skill and elegance is the place of the aura. This aura is less the product of the authenticity and unique existence of the object than the acknowledgment of its aesthetic and intellectual urgency (Benjamin 1968, 222–225).

In 1990s Syria cultural production was urgent for the state, for the intellectuals, and for the people who turned to the intellectuals to express their resistance. But the production of this culture was also much contested. Whoever succeeded in criticizing the regime with impunity risked being labeled complicit. It was the people's suspicion of the intellectuals that made the struggle so hard. How might they articulate resistance without being dismissed or absorbed?

In the next chapter I examine the dramatic strategies Saʿadallah Wannus and Mamduh ʿAdwan use to address vital issues in new and challenging ways. Their goal was to construct a public square where anything could be openly and, yes, freely discussed and where such discussions might have an impact beyond themselves.

You shall not escape us even while you sleep.
Your victims' vengeance will pursue you for blood . . .
Even if you muzzle their complaints they will haunt
   you even as ghosts . . .
You have poisoned the life of the people, wounded their
   souls.
—MAMDUH 'ADWAN, *The Ghoul*

chapter five

DISSIDENT PERFORMANCES

When we met at the end of May 1996 Sa'adallah Wannus was weakened by his disease and its savage treatment. But when he talked he seemed to forget himself. He reminisced about his role in Syrian theater and the various challenges he had faced in developing a national theater that would be entertaining, educational, and politically committed. He had been one of the key forces behind the biannual Damascus Drama Festival that operated from 1969 until 1988 and then resumed in the fall of 2004. He talked about his attempts since the 1960s to renew Arab theater through what he called *masrah al-tasyis*, or the theater of politicization.

He was writing for the popular classes, "whom the ruling powers crush so that they remain ignorant and apolitical. These are the classes that we hope will one day become the hero of the revolution and of transformation. *Tasyis* is an attempt to offer a progressive option to political theater" (Wannus 1996, 91). Tasyis is political, but it is also aesthetic; it is "not a ready-made grid but rather a framework for experimentation. . . . Its goal is to construct a new individual consciousness rather than deliver a ready-made communal consciousness" (93). This transformative work can not be accomplished through elite theater designed for the ruling classes with their "ready-made consciousness." The popular classes are more open to change because they can transform the subjective experience of anger and rejection into social, cultural, and political practice (106, 108). Masrah al-tasyis should compel people to reflect on their present and future, empowering them to "criticize and analyze hegemonic thinking that leads to defeat and its acceptance" (109). All drama, including historical theater, should engage the present in such a way that it creates a "new utterance [*qawl*] that truly reflects the concerns of its society and its time. And when this utterance comes into being we must find an artistic form that will accommodate and reveal it" (113, 124). This utterance is not only the words but also the dialogue they inspire and the action they incite. Dialogue became Wannus's mantra. Here is a blueprint for creative dissidence that will not be co-opted. Dissidence constitutes the first codification of an oppositional consciousness that may engage others and mobilize revolution. That is why it is so necessary and also so dangerous.

During the 1970s Sa'adallah was appointed director of the short-lived Experimental Theater and in 1977 he launched *Theatrical Life Magazine*, which he called an "Arab forum for critical theatrical thought." In 1979, after the closure of the Experimental Theater, he wrote for the National Theater and collaborated with Mamduh 'Adwan. In all, he wrote sixteen plays, the most critical of the regime during the last years of his life. In a situation where debate and imagination were stifled he hoped that his writings might help to raise people's consciousness about their situation: "Optimism can be drawn from a presentation of the mechanisms of frustration, despair and surrender" (Wannus 1996, 109). This kind of critical talk made the regime nervous.

Wannus's first major experiment was *An Evening's Entertainment for the Fifth of June* (1968), written a year after the 1967 War (in Wannus 1996, vol. 1, 21–127). At that time he believed "theater symbolized the birth of dialogue in society" that might extend the margins of democracy. He had hoped to "be able to do something about the oppressive instrument of power by implicating it in dialogue." First performed in 1971, the play questioned Syrian versions of the 1967 War that tried to put a positive spin on the defeat. Wannus made officials utter "windy victory speeches . . . but their rhetoric was interrupted by shouts of protest from the public. . . . These interventions came from actors seated offstage and were part of the play, but this was not evident to some members of the audience who tried to join in and had to be restrained. The play was a great success" (Seale 1989, 170–171). At that time audience participation was a brand-new concept.

When the poet Adonis praised him for his "technique," Wannus responded acidly, "What technique was he talking about? I wasn't looking for a technique or even for a way to renew the form. The political cause that I was confronting did not have any particular artistic shape. The form was in itself the content. The intensifying rhythm, for example, was the physical movement. The action. The form and the content were one. . . . Many categorized *An Evening's Entertainment for the Fifth of June* as a work of dramatic art and nothing more. In fact, it is a piece of writing and nothing more. Or, it is just a word structure. . . . The question I kept mulling was how to fashion this 'word/action'?" (1996, vol. 1, 238–239). Even though he later revised his earlier optimism about the power of the word, asserting that theater did not create revolution but only widened the spectator's horizon (115), Wannus still believed that theater, more than the other creative arts, might "launch a civil dialogue" that would shape a genuine civil society.

Performing Dissidence

In an authoritarian context, dialogue, or indeed any forum for the exchange of ideas, is so dangerous that it must be repressed. Dialogue creates an arena for subversive activity where individuals rethink their situations; civil dialogue allows dissidents to communicate the subjective experience of anger and rejection. Once the obstacles to self-awareness and its communication are overcome, revolution and transformation become possible.

In *Sun on a Cloudy Day* (published in 1973, three years after Hafiz Asad launched the Corrective Movement) Hanna Mina (b. 1924) identifies the first stirrings of creative dissidence and then explores the obstacles to its mobilization. Like Wannus, Mina proposes that it is only the popular classes who can transform dissidence into political action. Although it was written over twenty years before the period I am examining, this novel's interrogation of the social conditions compelling dissidence while constricting the possibilities for revolution are instructive.

Performance here provides a paradigm of dissident awakening and its struggle to go beyond itself. Mina's anonymous hero comes from the Francophile landed gentry, the colonized elite. In rebellion against his father he apprentices himself to a tailor-musician–revolutionary intellectual who persuades him to give up the Western violin for the Oriental lute, the tango for the dagger dance. Unexpectedly, our hero throws himself into the beat of the music, and he performs the most extraordinary dagger dance anyone has ever seen. When he is done, and the audience is still stunned, the tailor asks his pupil whether he had felt his heart beat wildly. No, he hadn't. The virtuoso performance puzzles the tailor. How could the dancer have felt nothing?

"To live for nothing is death. . . . Create something, even in your imagination. *Don't remain alone!*" (Mina 1973, 10; my emphasis). The tailor is calling for revolution and transcending the individual unthought moment of creative explosion to involve others. To have any kind of political meaning the dissident act must move beyond itself and implicate others.

What are we to make of the hero's total amnesia and his anxiety that he had lost a "part of [his] self" (Mina 1973, 18, 20)? The dissident dagger dance is a sublime performance of creativity that, Adonis writes, "is not horizontal, not a connected thread but rather moments and instants of staccato streams . . . a constant state of openness and a sense that perfection is a movement that cannot be perfected" (1974, 53). The performance functions outside ideology. The dissident act is not necessarily political, and therefore it need not lead to revolutionary practice. The task of the revolutionary is to channel the energy of the dissident so that it not dissipate, but become part of a dialogue that powers the engine of change. This is when the disciplinary mechanisms, what Wannus calls the "ready-made consciousness," of the ruling class intervene. In this case, the intervention is lethal. The hero's father kills the revolutionary tailor before he has the chance to fully win his son's allegiance. Dissidence is tolerable and, occasionally, useful; revolution is not. Class may not preclude dissident behavior, but it does block revolutionary engagement.

Dissidence is not agenda-driven but improvisational. It confronts and engages with dominant discourse. Always new and arresting, to survive, dissidence must deflect official attempts to repress it, reduce it to empty rhetoric, or co-opt it. While the critique is diffuse, the state will tolerate it. When it stumbles across the line drawn in secret ink, the line between dissidence and martyrdom, it is in the space of implication where it must be silenced or disappeared lest the individual impulse involve others.

How can revolutionary intellectuals survive? First of all, they must be part of the group they claim to represent. Second, their voices should not be theirs alone but the articulation of a group feeling, what the famous fourteenth-century North African world historian Ibn Khaldun called 'asabiya. This group feeling inheres in associations where individuals feel themselves bound to each other by blood or its equivalent: "Group feeling gives protection and makes possible mutual defence, the pressing of claims, and every other kind of social activity" (Ibn Khaldun 1969, 107). In his approach to dissidence and revolutionary leadership, Wannus was influenced by Ibn Khaldun's theories and also his life, which inspired one of his last and most important plays (see below).

In April 1995 foreign students at the French Institute were among the very few to stage Wannus's 1969 farce, *The Elephant, O King of Ages*, a play about inappropriate revolutionary leadership (1996, vol. 2, 451–477). The play tells the story of a royal elephant that wreaks havoc in a village and the attempt to stop him. Out of nowhere appears a certain Zakariya, who chastises the peasants for acquiescing to the king and his pet elephant. He takes charge of the situation and decides to lead the people to the king from whom they will demand restraint of the elephant. After vacillation and anxiety, the people agree to go. Granted a royal audience, they enter the gates and pass by the guards. Each step they take nibbles at their courage and daring. Finally, Zakariya faces the monarch and he can scarcely speak:

ZAKARIYA: The elephant . . .
KING: Yes?
ZAKARIYA: The elephant . . .
KING: Yes, what about the elephant!
ZAKARIYA: He needs a wife! (Wannus 1996, vol. 2, 475)

The words are out and the people's fate is sealed. The reckless intellectual with his bold agenda has become the agent of greater injustice when faced with the symbols of authority. Above all, he cannot represent the people because he is an outsider, and they are too weak and frightened to support him.

Wannus once said, "We create theater because we want change and development, and a deepening of communal consciousness about our historical destiny" (quoted in Sharif 1995, 260). He longed for a theater where history might be taught in defiance of the regime's attempts to erase the past. Such a theater would provide an arena for the construction of civil society because the erasure of "history is a key means for marginalizing civil society and encouraging the rule of tyranny. . . . Only a historical consciousness can extricate us from the vicious circle that blocks the road to the future" (262). In the early

1990s this historical consciousness pervaded the writings of Syrian intellectuals.

In his keynote speech at the 1996 World Theater Day (UNESCO, Paris), after being inducted into the International Academy for Theater, Wannus insisted that dramatic dialogue was an agent of transformation; it flourished in a climate that nurtured "democracy, respect for pluralism and control of the aggressive urge in individuals and nations alike. Every time I feel this thirst for dialogue, I imagine it starting in a theater [where] individuals can contemplate the human condition in a context that activates the sense of belonging to a community" (1996, vol. 1, 17–20). Dramatic dialogue that is both internal to the plot and also external, with the audience, creates the conditions for imagining change in a system opposed to change.

The Ghoul

On an early morning walk some time in late spring 1996 Mamduh 'Adwan and I were talking about how theater might become more politically effective.

"It's not enough to describe the jail cell," he said, "the breaking of the spirit must be dissected. It is not enough to describe the tyrant; we have to unmask the technology of tyranny in order to provide a way to counteract it and to turn frustration into optimism."

And this is what he does in his 1995 play *The Ghoul*.[1] He reveals on stage the deadly deceit of Jamal Pasha, the infamous Ottoman wali. This is a far cry from the licensed criticism that, Wedeen writes, tended not to challenge the president and his rule (1999, 92). The audience learns how a ruler like Jamal Pasha (or Hafiz Asad?) crafts a religious identity that allows him to perpetrate his crimes with seeming impunity (see introduction).

The Ghoul takes place toward the end of World War I when the French and the British were dividing the Middle East between them. It covers the trial of Jamal Pasha, the ruthless Ottoman governor in Syria. Notorious for his role in coordinating the extermination of Armenians and for mobilizing 100,000 men for the Safarbarlik that consumed so many lives, he now has to answer to his victims, who have returned from the land of the dead to bear witness.

Jamal Pasha makes light of the trial: "Do you think it will be easy for you to judge tyranny? . . . Tyranny is only tyranny once it has taken hold of its age. Hence, a trial of tyranny becomes a trial of the age that submitted to it" ('Adwan 1996, 30). The responsible are not only those who commit the evil, but those who let it happen. Isn't that what Havel said?

Jamal Pasha is at the center of a drama in the Middle East, with the Englishman Mark Sykes and the Frenchman Georges Picot carving out spheres of European influence. Dealing in 1916 with the "Jewish Problem," they become the architects of what is now called the "Middle East Problem." 'Adwan portrays them as buffoons who joke callously about the fragmentation of the Middle East.

Hated and distrusted, Jamal Pasha has to figure out some way of winning the people's trust. The Person, the keeper of the book of testimonies against him, advises him to be more publicly pious; he needs to work on his Muslim profile. The Ottoman governor protests that upon his arrival he did go to the mosque to pray, and the Person responds: "That's just the problem, Pasha. That was the only time you did pray."

In annoyance, Jamal mutters that he will pray, but that at the moment he is too busy. The Chorus responds, "Do not be surprised at what he says. You may know that the Ottomans who, for four hundred years ruled us in the name of Islam did not once make the Pilgrimage [to Mecca]" (61). Jamal Pasha realizes that he will have to try harder.

In a slapstick scene with the envoy from the Hashemite Sharif Husayn of Mecca, Jamal frantically adds the encomium "May God's prayers and blessings be upon him" to every mention of the name of the Prophet Muhammad (139–141). He uses his piety to justify his barbaric behavior, and he appeals to the Mufti As'ad al-Shuqayri, "Recite the verse!"

Given no further clue than "the verse," the Mufti has no idea which verse is meant. Jamal insists that the Mufti should know the verse:

"You don't remember! What do you remember then? If you can't remember a verse and you are the Grand Mufti, then who will? So, on top of everything else I am supposed to memorize the Qur'an? I have to do everything myself. This is your book, your Excellency the Mufti, your book written in your language" (194–196).

Toward the end of the play, noticing that Sharif Husayn's authority derives from the fact that he can trace his ancestry back to the Prophet, Jamal determines that he, too, will have such a lineage. To overcome the problem that there were no Turks connected with Muhammad, Jamal tells the Mufti of a vision:

> JAMAL: I saw, O God pray on the Prophet, a horseman with a green turban and a green waistcoat riding a green mare. Might this possibly be our Lord Khidr?
>
> AS'AD: Knowledge is with God.
>
> JAMAL: He stood in front of me just as you are standing right now and he said: Don't you recognize me? I froze, not knowing how to reply. So he added: You don't know me because you do not know yourself. Reveal your lineage. Do not leave the jewels hidden. Then he pulled at the horse's rein and left me in my confusion. My lord, how do you interpret all this?
>
> AS'AD: Knowledge is with God, Pasha. (223–225)

The Mufti is an unwilling accomplice and so the pasha coaxes him along, suggesting that Lord Khidr, the great Sufi guide of Moses (Qur'an 18: 61–84), was telling him that the two of them were linked. Each statement elicits from the dumbfounded mufti a "God knows," and then finally: "What do you want?"

The Pasha, it seems, wants "a Turkish wife or a slave girl who had been with God's Prophet . . . because she was my mother, Shaykh. My mother. Do you understand now?"

Yes, the Mufti understands. And now Jamal wants to know who she was. As'ad seems to give a little, saying, "I am not sure if the Prophet had a Turkish wife, and even if there had been a Turkish woman I am not convinced that she ever became pregnant." Undaunted, Jamal gives him his orders:

JAMAL: Make her pregnant, Shaykh. Make her pregnant!

AS'AD (nervously): Me, Pasha?

JAMAL: You. Someone else. It doesn't matter. (226–227)

He tells the Mufti to go to the history books, where all things may be found. He should dig up the genealogical chart, and then find a connection, the closer to the Prophet the better. When the Mufti turns in frustration to the Chorus to ask them what he should do, they repeat, "Make her pregnant." For if he does not, surely someone else will (231).

These farcical exchanges about Jamal Pasha's fabricated Muslim identity suggest dangerous parallels with Hafiz Asad's attempts to project a Muslim facade onto his Alawite identity (see introduction). The answer is to destroy the tyrant and the system he has put in place:

Wisdom at all times
Is to destroy the jail
Not to cut off the hand of the jailor.
We have completed our little duty
From now on we shall begin
our great duty:
This tyranny
shall never recur
shall never recur. (333–334)

These lines are a clarion call for revolution. The people must rise up against this tyranny so that it never recurs. It is not enough to cut off the hand of the jailor. The jail must be destroyed to disable the tyrant and eliminate tyranny.

Was this not dangerously political, I asked the night in November 1995 when 'Adwan invited a few of us over to his house to discuss the manuscript. There were eight of us in his little apartment in the Arab Writers Union building. Mamduh wanted feedback before it was published or performed.

"The play is historical," he said, "it's about tyranny in general."

I waited for someone else to comment on the contemporary relevance and the danger of so close a parallel to the president. No one said anything.

Months later and a few days before leaving, I met Mamduh to go through some of his poems and he reminded me of our preperformance dinner discussion.

"Too much time and energy," he said, "have been wasted confronting dictatorship directly. We believed that a poem could overthrow a dictator. We were enchanted with the thought that art is a weapon. Of course, it is. But it was not always like this. No poem, no piece of music can overthrow a dictator. But," he added reflectively, "it can resist the normalization of oppression. It can focus on human beings and their deep humanity, reminding them constantly that they are human. Artists must create works that will help others to understand what is going on and why and what is the possible outcome. When I wrote *The Ghoul* I was writing about Jamal Pasha, but beyond him I was writing also about the mechanism that creates dictators at all times and in all places." This sounded like a speech he'd prepared for a judge.

During the spring of 1996, the play was staged on several nights to a packed house at the popular Hamra Theater. The audience was thrilled at the daring language and the political allusions. Everyone declared *The Ghoul* to be an excellent portrayal of Jamal Pasha, even if the Sykes-Picot dialogues were a bit boring and pedantic. They had been able to breathe well (tanaffus) because in the space of the theater they had felt linked to each other in a community of dissidence. For that moment it did not matter that to breathe well risked renewed suffocation later. Their conscience had survived; they had resisted tyranny when they saw their resistance mirrored on the stage. The survival of individual dissidence and the popular conscience are interdependent.

This is the promise of theater: it empowers spectators to think the unthinkable. It opens up dialogue within and beyond the walls of the building. *The Ghoul*, like Czech theatrical performances in the 1970s, engaged spectators "grateful for every nuance of meaning, frantically applauding every knowing smile from the stage." The utopian promise of theater is that it throws together "the graveyard intentions of the powers that be [and] this irrepressible cultural hunger of the community's living organism, or perhaps that part of it which has not surrendered to total apathy" (Havel 1987, 125).

Historical Miniatures

Hope for change is vested in dissidents who dare to speak the unspeakable by drawing attention to oppression and injustice. Since words outlive actions, dissidents must choose carefully lest their daring be co-opted and serve only to uphold the system. According to anthropologist Katherine Verdery, intellectuals are essential to authoritarian regimes because they occupy "the 'space of legitimation,' a space of vital concern to a bureaucracy needing performances and compliance from its subjects" (1991, 88). Intellectuals do indeed have a vital role, and so they must beware lest they fall instead into the role of court jester.

Throughout his distinguished career Sa'adallah Wannus insisted that intellectuals implicate the regime and its ideologues in order to open a space for dialogue among the citizens. Their role was to create the conditions for action even when the obstacles seem insuperable. In 1990 Wannus looked back over twenty years, when "intellectuals had disappeared into prisons, exile and silence. Programs for revolutionary change have collapsed. Dialogue and discussion have stopped. Except for rare instances, writing has become a marginalized monologue heavy with frustration and despair" (1996, 583). Faced with punishment for speaking out, intellectuals were retreating into silence, and Wannus chided them for their disengagement.

In 1993, the year that he learned of his cancer, he published several scenes of his *Historical Miniatures* in the *Al-Safir* newspaper. This historical play concerns the encounter in 1400 between Tamerlane (d. 1405), the founder of the Timurid Dynasty from Samarqand, and Ibn Khaldun (d. 1406), the judge, historian, and proto-sociologist from Tunis. Reading Ibn Khaldun's own account of this momentous meeting from his autobiography and extrapolating from the theoretical propositions contained in his *Muqaddimah* (Introduction to history, written in five months in 1377), Wannus explored what might have been contemporary reactions to Ibn Khaldun's decision not to condemn the Tatar general and his lust for power.

The play begins when Tamerlane has raged across Asia and is advancing on Damascus. In the home of Shaykh Burhan al-Din al-Tadhili, the chief qadi of Damascus, Ibn Khaldun awaits the arrival of Sultan al-Nasir Faraj bin Barquq, the Mamluk ruler who has come from Egypt to confront the Tatar. During a meeting in the Umayyad Mosque, religious authorities deliberate whether to oppose the tyrant or to appease him. Encouraged by the presence of the Egyptian army that has stalled Tamerlane's merciless advance, they decide to issue a fatwa "calling for a *jihad* against the accursed Tamerlane, the enemy of God" (Wannus 1996, vol. 2, 336–342 [act 1, scene 4]).

Many fight and die but Ibn Khaldun feels only contempt, especially for those who do not count among the elite. Jihad is of no use against a force of nature like Tamerlane. Ibn Khaldun is in awe of this general who is so much greater than the ordinary men he has had the misfortune to serve, men who are "not worthy of being Tamerlane's shoes" (vol. 2, 417 [act 2, scene 8]). After meeting with him—a meeting that does not figure in the play—Ibn Khaldun advises the city elders to submit without a fight. Predictably, the citadel and its occupants are destroyed. Of this meeting, which Ibn Khaldun records in his autobiography, Mohamed Talbi writes, "Il n'est pas impossible qu'il a cru voir en lui l'homme du siècle disposant d'une *asabiyya* suffisante pour réunifier le monde musulman et imprimer un nouveau cours a l'histoire" (1973, 14).[2] To Ibn Khaldun the Tatars must have looked like the Bedouin civilization he described in the *Muqaddimah*. They were the raw energy of the desert unified by their group feeling and their loyalty to a charismatic leader. It was not so much Islamic unity or a new course for history that they portended, but rather the emergence of sublime power.

Fascinated by the potential realization of his twenty-three-year-old thesis of the rise and fall of civilizations, a cycle that begins with 'asabiya, the group feeling of Bedouin desert tribes, and ends in the decadence of urban culture, Wannus's Ibn Khaldun sees no point in trying to intervene in Tamerlane's project. He declares that since "the solidarity and group feeling of the Arabs have gone, *jihad* is no longer possible. No. No. Today *jihad* will only produce men tilting at windmills or wanting to deceive the world . . . those who consider themselves to be upholders of the truth and defenders against raiders and yet have no idea what kind of solidarity they need"; such folk are either crazy or liars (Wannus 1996, vol. 2, 394 [act 2, scene 3]). This is a time of decline and nothing can be done about it. In this civilizational sunset, the only glimmer of light comes from describing and bearing witness to the setting of the sun.

Ibn Khaldun separates knowledge from action because knowledge is superior and lasts longer. This is not mere fantasy on Wannus's part, but is derived from Ibn Khaldun himself. In the *Muqaddimah* we read that knowledge production and the ordering of things governing actions is human, and actions that are not "well arranged and orderly . . . are of living beings other than man. . . . The ability to think is the quality of man by which human beings are distinguished from other living beings. The degree to which a human being is able to establish an orderly causal chain determines the degree of his humanity" (Ibn Khaldun 1969, 334, 335).

Wannus questions the kind of knowledge Ibn Khaldun was producing. The historical determinism, the fatalism inherent in this thesis remains forever subject to scrutiny. What kind of knowledge is this that marginalizes and even denigrates action to the realm of the nonhuman? After six hundred years of respect, Ibn Khaldun is brought to task for his haughty abstention from action, for his political opportunism, and for his refusal to challenge the powerful Tamerlane. Wannus asks his audience to reflect on what the outcome might have been had Ibn Khaldun chosen to intervene. Ibn Khaldun was an extraordinary man who might have changed the course of history precisely because he was extraordinary. But this fourteenth-century genius was not interested in change, in evolution. He was interested in his theory and in survival.

Ibn Khaldun in life and in the play is an uncompromising pedagogue. With icy precision, he dismisses his student's sentimentality about the virtue of those who sacrifice themselves for the common good. Real scholars, he opines, must suppress the passion and excitement that corrupt insight and "objectivity" and write for posterity

(Wannus 1996, vol. 2, 359–362 [act 2, scene 8]). Scholars should not meddle in politics, but only describe, analyze, and stand apart from the turmoil of the present so that *future* generations may understand the events of the past.[3] To which his student responds, "We shall resist steadfastly until something in this nation changes. Something must change. If not, we shall have lost our right to exist." But right to exist or not, the rebellious student is saved because he is with Ibn Khaldun. The Tatar does not love Ibn Khaldun; he needs him to write a history of the Maghreb so vivid and detailed he could almost see it (vol. 2, 414–418). Although he knows why Tamerlane should want such a history, Ibn Khaldun agrees.[4]

The objective portrait of the tyrant may or may not move others to do something at the time, but it will provide a witness to a moment that might otherwise be lost. *Historical Miniatures* presents audiences with a conundrum: How should intellectuals react to injustice? Should they denounce it and actively oppose it? Or should they record their observations in a way that will allow others, more inclined to revolutionary actions perhaps, to speak out now or some time in the future?

Wannus is conducting a multiple critique against tyrants, disengaged intellectuals, and also unthought, suicidal reactions to injustice. Was Ibn Khaldun not right to save his skin and to give Tamerlane the book he commissioned? His objective descriptions and analyses have outlasted the passionate actions of those who died in the jihad to stop the deadly advance. His text, so close to unadorned reality, allows readers finding themselves in a comparable situation to decide what course of action to pursue. What is more, those whom he betrayed forgave him, and even history itself seems to have forgiven him. About the historical Ibn Khaldun, Talbi adds, "Après avoir rédigé pour Tamerlan une description du Magrib et avoir assisté aux horreurs de l'incendie et du pillage de Damas, il rejoignit le Caire . . . et, malgré son attitude compromettante vis-à-vis du chef mongol, il fut bien reçu à la cour" (1973, 14).[5] Neither the Damascenes nor the Cairenes considered Ibn Khaldun a traitor.

History has proven Ibn Khaldun right when he said to his student, "History will remember only the knowledge I have produced and the book I have written" (Wannus 1996, vol. 2, 418 [act 2, scene 8]). How are we today, six hundred years later, to deal with the fact that this is true? It is true that those who died fighting the tyrant have been forgotten and that the traitor survives as a hero. How are we to balance political commitment with literary survival?

Several intellectuals have deplored Wannus's negative portrayal of a Muslim hero. In June 1996 I met with the Syrian critic Riyad 'Ismat to discuss the play. He was appalled by the portrait Wannus had drawn. Assuming a direct parallel between Ibn Khaldun and those intellectuals who were selling out to normalization and to Israel, he lamented the compromised reputation of the great Arab world historian. Wannus was exploiting the immunity granted him by his Alawite identity; waxing lyrical, 'Ismat went on to denounce his later plays as derivative of European theater. For 'Ismat, Wannus was a court jester.

Ten years later I had another such encounter. In June 2006 in Algiers I gave a paper on the *Historical Miniatures* at the "Figures d'Ibn Khaldun: Réception, Appropriation, Usages" conference celebrating six hundred years since the death of Ibn Khaldun. Afterward, several participants denounced the play. The Moroccan historian and novelist Abdesalem Himmich upbraided me for not being more careful than Wannus. Did I not understand the fourteenth-century context? The notion of the intellectual, particularly the public intellectual, did not exist at that time. What could a mere scholar do to stop the savage devastations that were the hallmarks of Tamerlane's leadership style? Did I not know that Ibn Khaldun was not alone in making that fateful decision? He had acted morally when he had chosen the lesser of two inevitable evils. God only knows how absolute the destruction would have been had Ibn Khaldun not done what he did. When I appealed to Himmich's creative sensibilities and asked whether he did not believe that writers have the right to use facts, even well-known historical facts, to comment on the present and to project into the future, he shook his head vigorously. No, no one has the right to tarnish the reputation of Ibn Khaldun for current political purposes.

Unlike 'Adwan, Wannus did not deny the connection between the fourteenth-century historian and contemporary Syrian intellectuals.

History as the *past*, he told Mahir al-Sharif, "was not at all my pre-occupation" (al-Sharif 1995, 264). But history as *future* was, because "however horrible the defeat and the massacre, they will not stop the flow of history. Hence, hope is possible despite everything" (265). Yes, theater is the special place where author, director, actors, and audience together turn history into a new utterance that truly reflects the concerns of its society and its time.

On stage, Wannus allows spectators to decide for themselves whether they believe that the great man did the right thing. But in interviews he was unequivocal: "Knowledge entails a responsibility. Intellectuals should intervene in public affairs and oppose aggressors as well as tyrannical rulers. . . . I was not demanding of Ibn Khaldun what might appear strange in his time" (Sharif 1995, 266, 269). He had to act even though he could not "come to a satisfactory accommodation between practice and writing. Today, things are increasingly difficult, because those who believe in writing [for its own sake] hold sway in the cultural sphere. They are making known their contempt for mixing activism, creativity and history" (270). Writing is inherently political for Wannus. Whoever stands by enables the tyrant.

In his review of this play, 'Abd al-Rahman Munif called Ibn Khaldun "one of the greatest, most confused, most ambitious, and most wicked adventurers in Arab history" (1996, 125–126). He was harsher than Wannus, who seems more sad than angry to discover the man behind the legend. Munif related this six-hundred-year-old story to today. Exposing the gaps in the fantasy of freedom and taking the nationalist slogan "Culture Is Humanity's Highest Need" at its word, Munif wrote that culture

> must serve humanity and its happiness. . . . Its function is not merely to explain events, but to implant values, behaviors, traditions and a vision whose goal is to inspire respect for what is true, noble and enlightening in human life and history. It should lead to progress and well-being in all spheres and not only in one sphere at the expense of the other. . . . *There is no neutrality in culture. The intellectual cannot be impartial . . . but must be completely engaged in the present epoch, using culture to influence*

the times. . . . . There must be coordination and equivalence between words and their meanings . . . .. If not, these words will turn into curses and the one who is best versed in this craft will be the most dangerous. . . . This is what has made many instrumentalize their knowledge and skills on behalf of the state. . . . This is what has made them wealthy whatever their motives." (1996, 118, 131; my emphasis)

Intellectuals have a moral authority they must not abuse because, like a beast of prey, the state is lying in wait ready to pounce on those it can use. Intellectuals should challenge official mystifications. Munif is responding to Žižek's proposal that intellectuals take the power discourse at its word, acting as if it really means what it says and promises. Munif's words echo those of 'Adwan's Chorus when they warn that deceptive words will turn into curses and "the victims' vengeance will haunt you."

Munif knew how heavy was the price to be paid for defying a regime. Born in Saudi Arabia, he forfeited his citizenship for daring to criticize the kingdom of oil, and he ended his days in Damascus. Munif confirmed Wannus' lament: "The times are indeed dark. More than at any other time probably we are in need of enlightened intellectuals who do not shirk their responsibilities and who fully confront this darkness and its brutalizing force" (Wannus, quoted in Sharif 1995, 274–276). Wannus assumed the responsibility that Ibn Khaldun shirked by writing works of extreme daring, tying words to their meanings and to the actions they might incite.

Sa'adallah Wannus wrote despite the danger that the regime might stop providing medical care or, perhaps worse, coopt his dissident voice. For the last three years of his life, he had to accept government help to finance his cancer treatment. He risked the charge that he was in its pay and that his criticism had been licensed, that he had become a muharrij, or court jester.

Was Wannus like Eastern European intellectuals before 1989 with whom the regime tried to come to terms "by persistently ascribing utilitarian motivations to them—a lust for power or fame or wealth" (Havel 1987, 62)? I doubt that Wannus lusted for power or fame or wealth, but he would have died sooner and he would not have been able to write his final, highly critical plays without government support. He was trying to make a difference, to live in truth, while daily risking his ability to do so. His writings and their reception proclaim their worth and the high esteem in which he was held. Would seventy thousand people have attended the funeral of a court jester?

Wannus's condemnation of Ibn Khaldun's abrogation of political responsibility challenges us in the United States, with its war on terror that is becoming a war on those who critique that war. In this great democracy freedom of thought is in jeopardy. It sometimes seems useless to protest, to speak truth to this unjust system. What difference can mere academics, ivory tower intellectuals make in Bush's United States? Sa'adallah tells us that we can make a difference and that intellectual acquiescence to an unjust state leads to destruction. Munif was right: there is no neutrality in culture.

What happens to a dream deferred?

Does it dry up
like a raisin in the sun?
Or fester like a sore—
And then run?
Does it stink like rotten meat?
Or crust and sugar over—
like a syrupy sweet?

Maybe it just sags
like a heavy load.

Or does it explode?
—LANGSTON HUGHES,
"Dream Deferred"

chapter six

FILMING DREAMS

On 30 October 1995 the ninth biannual Damascus Film Festival brought in filmmakers from Asia, Africa, and Latin America and transformed the dull downtown into vibrant activity. The festival kicked off in the sumptuous theater of a Cham Palace Hotel somewhere outside town. The chic and famous of Syrian high society and glamorous international filmmakers and actors were there for the premiere of *Su'ud al-matar* (Rising rain) by one of Syria's best-known directors, the Alawite 'Abd al-Latif 'Abd al-Hamid.

A writer in his garret struggles to keep a check on his wild imagination. Seated in front of his typewriter he starts to tap out the story of two lovers he observes on the roof of a building across the road. No sooner does he start to write their story than his mind conjures up dangerous visions and dreams. Suddenly, a hailstorm of watermelons crashes on the pavement and street below, their sweet red juice transformed into what looks like the blood of a massacre. One huge watermelon does not fall but floats down lightly. Out steps a clown who mischievously drags the writer away from the love story he is writing to rallies and demonstrations. How, the clown wants to know, will the writer develop his role? Jerked back into reality, the writer escapes his typewriter and wanders around the building trying to shake the nightmare. Torn between a safe story about a couple meeting surreptitiously and the ghouls of his imagination, he cannot write. He lives in a night world over which he has no control.

What more powerful evocation of the terror inherent in self-censorship? 'Abd al-Hamid had produced a brilliant example of what film critics Ella Shohat and Robert Stam have called "carnivalesque subversions" (1994, 302–306). The film ends when the little heater in his study explodes and he is killed. But death does not stop his writing. Some time after the funeral his grave opens up to disgorge the writer, who is still typing madly on his muddy machine. The dissident intellectual cannot be stopped. Writing as a ghost is easier than writing alive, even if in both cases the text will not be read. 'Abd al-Hamid had exposed the horrors for a creative writer of life under authoritarian rule, where the greatest enemy is one's own treacherous imagination and death is the only safe place to write. Like 'Adwan's tyrant who does not die when he dies, so the dissident lives on to speak truth to power.

When we filed out of the theater, I overheard the rapturous comments: the actors . . . the photography . . . the lighting. How, I wondered, could the jury award the silver medal to such a radical film? (President Hafiz Asad as usual was awarded first prize.) My surprise that this daring film should be honored was met with blank looks. What did I mean, "daring"? It was a beautiful film, if a bit confusing.

The Extras

Parallel to the official festival the organizers had programmed a side festival devoted to Syrian cinema. Movies much discussed but seldom, if ever, seen were shown in the older theaters away from the center.[1] Long lines would start forming around two hours before the show was due to start. The intense interest in Syrian films belied the official position that domestic films were not popular. In fact, Syrians liked their national films very much, appreciating their claustrophobic cinematography, the allegorical plots, and the sometimes political language that led to bans or disappearance of films that the government had sponsored.

During the 1995 festival, two Syrian films drew large crowds: Nabil Malih's prize-winning 1993 *Al-kumbars* (The extras) and Muhammad Malas's *Al-layl* (Night). *The Extras* tells the deceptively simple story of a couple's two-hour tryst. Nada, a young widow living with her brother and his family, is in love with Salim, a garage attendant with hopes of a career in the theater. Too poor to marry and live alone, they meet in parks and alleys. One day, they use the garçonniere of Adel, Salim's friend, for two hours. In the filthy apartment with its decrepit furniture, tension mounts. This is the first time the lovers will have met alone. Salim is anxious for Adel to leave and jumpy about sounds in the hallway. Suddenly, a suspicious-looking man in a suit sticks his nose around the door. Without introducing himself or providing proof of his right to barge in, he looks around the hallway:

ADEL: Can I help you?

MAN: Just a routine, simple question. Nothing important. No problem.

Adel holds on to the door, clearly distressed. The man keeps looking over his shoulder at Salim:

MAN: Haven't we met before?

SALIM: No, I've not had the honor.

MAN: Do you know the man next door, the blind lute player?

Salim and Adel stutter and hesitate, fearing that anything they say might implicate them in some crime they had not known they had committed. While Salim hallucinates an attack on the interloper, Adel assures the man that he does not know the musician. Salim, however, stammers that he had heard him play for a party they attended. The man in the suit notes the inconsistency and rushes out as abruptly as he had entered. The weight of his suspicion lingers long after he is gone.

SALIM: Who was he?

ADEL: When people look like that you don't have to ask their identity because it is stamped on their face.

Adel leaves and Salim waits, his hyperactive imagination conjuring up orgies, an attack on the informer, and then Nada's brother coming to kill him.

When Nada finally arrives, she, too, is trembling with fear, sure that her brother saw her enter the building. Salim tries to calm her, but he cannot stop himself from asking, "Did you see a man on the stairs?" She is terrified: What man?! The stairwell, as Adel told Salim, was a vertical street with people constantly on the move. Salim pretends that all is well: isn't it wonderful that they are finally alone in a place where they "have nothing to do with what is happening out there"? But wishful thinking cannot overcome their terror of what is happening out there: the strains of the blind man's lute float through the wall. The sound of the lute that came to connote danger. Nada senses Salim's fear; she is anxious to leave the confinement of the apartment because "the world outside is more merciful." People, she muses, "have thousands of things they want to say but they die without being able to say them. Life passes as though through a desert."

The tragedy of life wasted, stolen, hangs heavy over the couple as they struggle to enjoy this reprieve in their policed relationship. To break the gloom, Salim decides to act out for Nada the seven roles he has in a current play: a citizen, a soldier, a beggar, a thief, a guard, a demonstrator, and an informer: in each "I die upon request." When Nadia asks what he'll think if she does not like the play, Salim shoots back, "You know better than the director of the National Theater?" How could she imagine, even only for a moment, that she might have her own opinions? Public opinion cannot but reflect state ideology.

Salim acts out some of his roles and he asks Nada to play the tyrant so that he can respond defiantly to her insults; she should then throw him into prison for insubordination. Unexpectedly, Adel's girlfriend bursts in and turns the place upside down. Imparting little lessons about the cost of love and how only the rich can afford to indulge it, she leaves. With a sigh of relief, they fall on the bed, which promptly collapses. A brief moment of farce alleviates the growing tension. Nada crawls under the bed to hold up the frame so that Salim can reconstruct the bed. The bed is too heavy and Salim joins her. Shot-reverse-shot gives way to a new perspective, with the camera moving above the couple squeezed in under the bed wires to assume the point of view of a voyeur looking down on two prisoners caged together. The camera remains still, almost as though it was a hidden surveillance mechanism relaying images to someone, perhaps to the man in the suit, the informer.

NADA: Can you imagine people living for year3s behind such wires?!
SALIM: Prison wires are different (Salim replies as though from experience). Each bar is thick like this (and he stretches his arms as widely as the bed wires will let him). Some people are imprisoned without bars and wires!

Note the change from wires to bars. These people that Salim imagines imprisoned without bars are people are like them, ordinary Syrians who may find that they are safe only behind bars. And for Nada and Salim, too, this prison is the only place where they feel safe enough to touch, if only for a moment. The word "prison" is a leitmotiv in Salim's play and also in the film.

The clay figures in "The Variety of Citizens' Rights" provide a striking illustration of this confinement of daily life that could have been taken from Malih's film. In this image, bloated people lounge around a conference table while prisoners float above as if in a thought bubble. Those prisoners, held in by wires, exactly like those that cage the luckless lovers in *The Extras*, mock the empty text that details

"The Variety of Citizens' Rights." In Abbas and Maala,
Citizenship Guide (2005), p. 32.

citizens' rights: "Freedom of expression, freedom of assembly, freedom to join organizations. These freedoms are both individual and collective. . . . These rights may be connected with personal security, including protection from arbitrary arrest or imprisonment" ('Abbas and Maala 2005, 33). These freedoms and the right to protection from arbitrary imprisonment are mocked by the imprisoned people. Returning to the film, we see the lovers prepare to leave, their attempts at intimacy having failed. To their horror, the man in the suit bursts in looking for the musician. They were not crazy to be paranoid.

The play ends with the informer returning to drag away the lute player, who has no idea what crime he has committed. This last image suggests the intellectual punished for his art and his ideas. This was the condition of life in 1990s Syria for the intellectuals but often also for the people in the street.

Despite the fact that it did not touch on any of the cinema taboos (the president, certain political events, religion), the film, which had been financed by the National Film Organization, was banned, a guarantee of its popularity. During the Syrian sideshow at the 1995 Damascus Film Festival, *The Extras* played to a full house.

Dreaming Features

The greatest excitement, however, surrounded a three-year-old film. It was Muhammad Malas's *Night*. It was to be screened for the first time in an old uncomfortable theater away from the downtown where all the new films were being shown. We had been waiting for over an hour in a long line snaking around the block. There was something wrong with the film or the projector or something. But no one thought of leaving. When the doors finally opened around midnight, the audience filed in tensely, suspicious of everyone because of the plainclothes police. They knew their presence was being noted and recorded and that their participation might serve as testimony against them whenever necessary. To attend such a film was an act of political daring. Shohat and Stam have written that when "a repressive regime makes film going a clandestine activity punishable by prison or torture, the mere act of viewing comes to entail political engagement" (1994, 262).

Born in Kuneitra in Syria's Golan Heights in 1945, Malas was three when the state of Israel was established and twenty-two during the 1967 War, when the Israelis attacked and occupied his hometown. What he saw and experienced there marked him profoundly. After graduating in 1974 from VGIK, the Moscow Film Academy, Malas started to turn his tortured memories into what some critics have called "visual poetry."[2] The cinematography of Syria's first *auteur de cinéma*[3] mixes dreams, individual memories, and national history in such a way that they interrogate each other. Malas once said that cinema "represents a personal means of expression, and not a profession that is supposed to secure me material or moral profit. [My films] are related to me as a human being and individual, but also as a product of a whole generation, of a specific epoch, of a society, and a country" (quoted in Shafik 1998, 185).

His two feature films, *City Dreams* (1984) and *Night* (1991),[4] received the prestigious Tanit d'Or at the Carthage Film Festival. *City Dreams* also received the Golden Palm in the 1984 Valencia Film Festival and it was the first Arab film ever to be included in the Cannes Critics' Week. In 1992 *Night* was the first Arab film to be picked for the New York Film Festival. While both films were widely reviewed in the Arab and European presses, at home they were not even acknowledged. The government that had sponsored their making forbade their screening.[5]

In his documentaries Malas probes the memories of people who have nothing left but their dreams, or rather, their nightmares. Each film, whether feature or documentary,[6] reflects on the meaning of identity, loss, dispossession, and amnesia. Malas paints the canvas of his fin de siècle society, courageously pointing at the forbidden, compelling others to acknowledge the disappearance of places, and evoking the violence of their disappearance.

Telling dark stories that blur the boundary between national and familial violence, *City Dreams* and *Night* are connected through Wissal, a woman who is the wife of a freedom fighter and the mother of the boy narrator. The mystery driving both plots is the father's death and the anxiety about who killed him.

City Dreams begins with a bloody coup in the early 1950s and celebrations ushering in a new regime. It is followed by independence parades, wars, reprisals against religious extremism, people run over by tanks, people drowning in the Barada River, and Muslim Brothers (a warning of the 1982 Hama massacre of Muslim Brothers) shouting "Down with Nasser!" and "Down with Adib Shishakli!" Prisoners are rounded up. The quickly changing portraits of presidents in shop windows gesture to the succession of coups. While the butcher applauds each new dictator, young men shout slogans for one new leader after the other.

"Fuck this country," one man says, "you go to bed with one regime and awake with another."

This is the background to the departure of the war widow Wissal with her two sons from Kuneitra. They are bound for her father's place in Damascus. The mean old man resents his daughter and sends the younger boy to an orphanage and the older, Dib, to work in a laundry. Dib observes with detachment people's cruelty to each other. He is not old enough to participate or to comment in a way that might be identified as transgressive because his witness appears innocent and politically neutral. Through the steam, he watches men and women slaving in the laundry, a man killing his brother, his grandfather tormenting his family, and his mother wishing that she and her sons were dead: "Not even an enemy," she yells at her father, "would do what you have done!"

Like many other heroines of late twentieth-century Asian films, Wissal seems to represent "the failures of national ideals or movements. These nationalist dramas portray women as powerful, though ultimately vulnerable and defeated, while the men are uniformly ineffectual, manipulative, callous and evil. . . . The women serve to mediate the historical span that links the diegetic past to the filmmaking present, the past being the displaced site of the tensions, failures and anxieties of the present" (Chakravarty 2003, 80–81).

City Dreams ends with the fanfare of the 1958 union with Egypt and the anthem "Nothing Can Defeat the Union." In the empty city a lone man shouts, "Do you see the moon! Even God is with the Union!" The bleak sloganeering and deserted streets hint that right from the start no one had believed in the Union that was to collapse three years later.

When Malas asked me to help with the English subtitles, I happily agreed. We had met at the French Institute in October. A quiet man, he has sleepy, sad eyes that sparkle when he is excited. During the spring of 1996 I spent two afternoons a week with him and his wife in their one-room basement apartment near Rawda Square in the embassies district. They had moved there in 1992 after a run-in with the National Film Organization over the financing of *Night* (see below). The building was across the street from one of Hafiz Asad's palaces that was guarded day and night by men in jeans, black leather jackets, and sunglasses. Every time I went there the men would turn and stare. Malas and his wife were living under virtual house arrest. I would walk down a flight of stairs into the black of the well and knock at the door. The place was dark; its only windows were high slits at ground level and the dim light they let in even at midday had to be supplemented with electric light.

After we had been working together for several weeks on the subtitles to *Dreams*, I felt comfortable enough to ask about the equivalence between the grandfather and Hafiz Asad. It was as if a shutter had been pulled down between us.

"The point of metaphors," Malas said, suddenly cool, "is not to provide answers but to make people think." I felt rebuked but also instructed. Political interpretation does not always have to be trumpeted. Yes, metaphors are to make people think.[7] Censorship, which Malas had once called a gift because it "forces one to look for new and more interesting structures through which to speak" (Porteous 1995, 209), had shaped the metaphorical nature of his filmmaking.

Outside Syria, Malas was more open. After *City Dreams* had won first prize at Valencia's 1984 Fifth Mostra del Cinema Mediterrani, he gave an interview to the Spanish *Hoja del Lunes de Valencia* about the political climate in which he had to work: "There is rigorous state control at every level: production, distribution and screening. . . . This situation imposes tough conditions on the freedom of expression. Every day I wonder whether it's worth continuing to make films under such circumstances. Yet I go on because there is always hope." He could still hope because he knew he was getting through to viewers, providing "a mirror allowing each person to see their own memories. . . . Films can make up for the deficiencies of memory" (quoted in Tawq 1993, 50). The memory comes alive when it is apprehended through the correspondence between sight and sound and their impression stored in memory. This Proustian correspondence animates other senses, especially smell: "My son," the mother whispers, "we pick an instant from life and this instant has its own perfume."

This instant, Malas has said, is "when sound [sawt] and image [sura] come together harmoniously. It is when faithfulness to the memory of a sound and an image harmonizes with my reflections on memory and produces a narrative language" (Tawq 1993, 50). Sight, sound and smell work together to revive the repressed memory.

Set in Kuneitra some time between 1936 and 1987, Night is dedicated to those, like the boy's father, "who fought for Palestine and who died unacknowledged and in silence."[8] The narrator is sometimes the child whose father has just died and sometimes the adult looking back on that period of confusion. Reality, dream, and memory melt into each other to project new memories that overlay other memories so shattered and repressed that they press the present into the black of night. In its relentless darkness Night recalls other Syrian films of the 1980s and early 1990s that take place at night. The almost black screen provides cover for clandestine movements. All the spectator may distinguish is a profile thanks to the faint flicker of a candle or a figure running through a wood betrayed by the shimmer of moonbeams on wet leaves.

Night is the time for fugitives to feel free, even if not safe. Night is the time for dreams that create "a realm beyond the bounds of censorship, ideology or even self-consciousness" (Porteous 1995, 212), where alternative realities can be imagined. Dreams are a "site of subterfuge . . . through which the 'dreamer' can simultaneously articulate political criticisms and disavow responsibility for them" (Wedeen 1999, 72); they are at the very source of dissidence and that is why they are forbidden. Others have also explored the crime of dreaming,[9] agreeing with Oscar Wilde that "society often forgives the criminal; it never forgives the dreamer" (quoted in Williams 1983, 170). Present, future, and past become one; they are the stones that build the house of a nation in which he can root himself. Dreams turn memory into a new critical reality.

Night interrogates the destruction of two cities, Kuneitra in 1967 and Hama in 1982, that have receded into the back of public memory, leaving absences that individuals fill at their own peril. However, dangers notwithstanding, Malas has visited these *lieux de mémoire*, what Pierre Nora calls both an event (time) and a place that "occurs when an immense and intimate fund of memory disappears, surviving only as a reconstituted object beneath the gaze of critical history" (quoted in Slyomovics 1998, 4).

This dream film begins at night somewhere in Kuneitra when Wissal calls her son to recount a dream about his father. Malas creates what film critic Stephen Heath calls a "dream screen, the blank surface present in dreams though mostly 'unseen,' covered over by the manifest content of the projected dream." This is the "master shot" that will "allow the scene to be dominated in the course of its reconstitution narratively as dramatic unity" (1976, 23, 25).

The boy listens intently and in the black we can distinguish only the shade of a profile. Is it the boy who is listening or is this a flashback to his father? When Wissal is done speaking, the screen brightens and the image sharpens into the present. She asks her son to put flowers on his father's tomb, wherever it might be. The boy goes off into the night, and when he does not return, she follows him. The boy's search and that of his mother converge in a lieu de mémoire, the village mosque. This is where, one day in 1936, his father had passed on his way to fight for Palestine, the place where he may have died (or been killed). Twice his father fought for Palestine and twice Syrian authorities imprisoned and finally disappeared him.

The boy wanders through Kuneitra, the streets represented in jarring shots. In search of traces of a repressed history, the camera peeps through the shattered glass of windows to see "what no human eye is capable of catching, no pencil, brush, pen of pinning down" (Bresson

1986, 26). Events emerge out of "nothing, out of night, out of this primal mystery made of silence. Myth produces history, dream produces reality, and silence produces the world" (Chikhaoui 1995, 9).[10]

Sudden and unannounced shifts from one historical moment to another hurl the viewer into the confusion of the boy's and mother's memories: "Whenever she told me her story about my father's death," says the boy in voice-over, "I would tell her mine of the death I wanted for him. She would not say anything as though questioning memory and imagination, casting them into doubt."

Night probes the dark recesses of national pride and official history. Like Wannus's *An Evening Entertainment for the Fifth of June*, this film plays with the forbidden, questioning what actually happened during the Israeli occupation of Kuneitra in 1967 and suggesting that what lies "behind the occupation is uglier," to cite the title of a review of the film. Official amnesia covers over the deeds of the state. During the night of Syrian sleep the "memory of the people can feel nothing, not even the pain of amnesia" (Shakir 1996, 20). In such a context even the shards of shattered memories, like those of the mother, begin to build an archive that can help revise official versions.

"*Night*," Malas told Jean al-Kassan (1992), "is a memory film in terms of concept, content, medium and substructure. This memory needs to be tested, to be put in the witness stand. The film is not about memory. It *is* memory itself." Memory weaves together the strands of dream and reality to create the texture of a newer, truer history, a kind of living testimonial. In the fragments of his mother's memory, the boy searches for the truth about his father. He has to distinguish between what he is told, what is suggested, and what he wants: "another death for him. One that will do him honor; his father will oppose the Israeli occupation and will die a martyr. This desired death allows the author to cleanse his father and his destroyed city of the shame of memory" (Kassan 1992).

Picking up clues that will help him solve some of the many mysteries that haunt his present, the boy pieces together a past he can inhabit. So, who killed patriots like his father, *al-muta'adhdhib fi qabrihi*, the one tortured in his grave? Who destroyed the city? Was it the Israelis or the Syrians? Although clearly *Second* Cinema, with

Night's splintered dreams.

its focus on "intellect and interiority . . . [and not] political radical-ism" (Guneratne and Dissanayake 2003, 10), *Night* is also what Sho-hat and Stam have called a "post–Third Worldist" film that displays a "certain skepticism toward metanarratives of liberation, but do not necessarily abandon the notion that emancipation is worth fighting for. But rather than fleeing from contradiction, they install doubt and crisis at the very core of the films" (1994, 288).

Night takes on the forbidden with absolute conviction. The forbid-den here is 1967 Kuneitra but also 1982 Hama. In *Night* the refer-ences to the destruction of the old city and the massacre are made visually and symbolically explicit through the representation of *no-rias*, the ancient Roman water wheels. The *noria*, metonym for Hama, has become the sign of the massacre.

No writer in his right mind was touching Hama. Literary critic Mohja Kahf has written that Syrian literature "contains no account of the Hama massacre. . . . The silence on Hama is notable, given the sophisticated levels of political consciousness among Syrian writers. An episode of this magnitude in a country's third largest city does not just pass unnoticed by the country's major poets and novelists, no matter what their ideological leanings" (2001, 229).

Maybe writers had kept silent, but the filmmaker Malas had not. A collage of water wheels links Hama with Kuneitra, the two homes of the martyred father and each a taboo site of state violence against its people. A native of Hama, the father passed through Kuneitra on his way to and from fighting with the Palestinians. It was in Kuneitra that he married. When the shadow of the water wheels falls on the streets of Kuneitra, the two cities destroyed within fifteen years of each other are linked: 1967 and 1982 interrogate one another.

This connection was not lost on critics. In Jurj Kaadi's interview with Malas for the Beirut newspaper *al-Nahar*, he writes sardonically, "In *Night* water wheels connect Kuneitra and the city to which the principal character of the film belongs. I mean Hama with its water wheels and its good air" (1992). Zinelabidine Benaissa has noted the association not only in the title of his critical essay, "The Waterwheel, Water and Wind," but also in the recurrence of the name throughout the film: "Hama, whose name returns casually in a conversation or in voice over . . . relates what one sees to what one guesses." He gestures toward the equivalence without ever mentioning it openly. What matters, he concludes, is not the repressed event, however bloody, but how it is represented (1995, 15–16). Malas had been unusually transparent in his criticism of the regime.

It was not only the politics of the film that got Malas into trouble, it was also the filming and funding. Why? The National Film Organization (NFO) was the only institution that could commission the production of films. Since every stage in the production and direction was submitted to the Censor Board, the NFO knew everything about the films it owned and distributed. The NFO might commission a film but then disable its completion by denying sufficient funding and forbidding filmmakers to seek outside sponsorship. This way of dealing with film production has earned the NFO the title *maqbarat al-aflam wa al-sinima'iyin*, "the graveyard of cinema and filmmakers."

When Malas sought external funding to complete the production of *Night* he committed what the Ministry of Culture called a crime. In 1989, with his two closest associates, Umar Amiralay and Usama Muhammad, he formed MARAM, a private film company that coproduced *Night* and in 1992 printed it in Paris. Despite its subvention of the film, the NFO did not permit its screening in Syria, accusing it of being "an attack on militarism in general and the Syrian military in particular." Undeterred, Malas bypassed the NFO and in 1993 sent prints of the film to foreign film festivals. In April 1994, the NFO told the Syrian Embassy in Ankara to pull *Night* from the Istanbul Film Festival. Malas was denied permission to travel. In early June, he drafted a public complaint about this harassment. Twelve artists and intellectuals signed the document, which they faxed to the Institut du Monde Arabe in Paris and to Radio Monte Carlo. In retaliation, the Ministry of Culture charged MARAM with administrative and financial improprieties. On 14 June 1994 Marwan Haddad, director of the NFO, called a press conference to present the government's position: the NFO had financed 88 percent of the film and MARAM only 12 percent, yet Malas and Amiralay had sold rights to British and Swiss television networks. The case was referred to the Economic Security Court, where petty crimes are usually adjudicated. The court found

Malas and Amiralay guilty and put out a warrant for their arrest. Within five days, on 19 June, the Institut du Monde Arabe in Paris awarded Malas a 20,000-franc prize for *Night*. A provocation to the Syrian state, the prize had the desired effect. Najah Attar, the minister of culture, arranged for the case against him to be dropped. International publicity had worked this time.

When I asked him about the court's order to freeze his assets, Malas laughed: "I have no assets, liquid or nonliquid, so the court decision did not affect me. That was not the point. They wanted to make us look like thieves in order to cow opposition intellectuals."

Documenting Dreams

Palestine before Israel in the night world of refugees in Palestinian camps in Lebanon is the subject of *Dream* (1987). *Dream* recounts the imaginary of survivors through the dreams of Palestinians living in the Lebanese camps of Sabra, Shatila, Burj al-Barajna, Ain al-Hilwa, and al-Rashidiya. Between 1980 and 1981, Malas lived in the camps and interviewed more than four hundred people. Hovering over the lines separating dream and memory from reality, and dissidence from martyrdom, his camera dives into the subconscious where hopes and fears and sadness coexist.

"The world was the color of light," says one woman. "They were saying we'd won. And I said: Unbelievable! So quickly!"

"I dreamt of a bombardment and the earth was trembling," a *fida'i* (freedom fighter) remembers, "houses were collapsing and people dying. . . . I picked up a two-year-old and started to run. I was shot in the chest but there was no blood and I kept on running." Another Palestinian dreams of a meeting with Gulf emirs who ignore him.[11]

In *The Dream: A Film Notebook* (1991), Malas writes about his meetings in Burj al-Barajna, 'Ain al-Hilwa (near Sidon), and Sabra and Shatila before the massacre of 1982. The *Notebook* reveals how each story dictated cinematographic choices. In a room hung with pictures of Che Guevara, Arafat, and young people, Malas hesitated to ask the parents about their children. The aching sadness was everywhere, but in some cases it was so intense that it alone became the story, like Abu Shakir, whose eyes were swollen from incessant weeping. Malas told his dream through the eyes of the old man. The camera moves from Malas' perspective with a close-up of Abu Shakir's eyes and then assumes the point of view of the old man from the moment he closes his store to his return home to his going to bed (18–20). Like a fiction film, this documentary blurs the "supposed boundaries between fact and fiction, art and reality, documentary and creativity" (Porteous 1995, 212). The film constructs "the psychology of dispossession; the daily reality behind those slogans about nationhood, freedom, land and resistance, for people who have lost all of these things except their recourse to the last" (213).

The first stage of filming was completed in September 1981. Then in June 1982 the Israelis invaded Lebanon and besieged Beirut and the camps, and some of the people he had interviewed were killed.

"I was paralyzed with grief and anxiety for the friends I had made," he said. "I had to do something else and so I turned my attention to *City Dreams*."

The critical success of his first feature film gained Malas the sponsorship necessary to complete the shooting. In 1987, *Dream* won first prize at the Cannes International Audio Visual Festival (FIPA). Malas noted that it has scarcely ever been screened while *Trotsky*, which won second prize, "has been distributed around the world."

Another documentary shot at a lieu de mémoire is *Chiaroscuro*. It is about Nazih Shahbandar, whom Malas calls Syria's first filmmaker.[12] In the early 1930s, when Hollywood was coming into its own, a modest Syrian engineer invented a way of "recording voice with light." Malas' tenderness toward this broken old man is that of a son for his beloved father whose dreams have crumbled. One afternoon, before turning on his own crumbling tape of this documentary, Malas spoke sadly about Shahbandar and his destroyed film.

"He was a pioneer, an engineer without a degree, and his only film shot since independence in 1947, *Chiaroscuro*, was burnt. He kept the burnt celluloid, periodically taking it out and looking at it. When I filmed him, he was still living in the set he'd built for the film over forty years ago." The walls were disintegrating; the windows were broken.

Only seven precious minutes survive. Malas punctuates Shahbandar's story of a young man in an egg-shaped spaceship who comes to earth in search of paradise and finds hell, with rolling screens of dusty, charred celluloid strips that appear to be touched for the first time in over forty years. These frames recall *Night* when Wissal and her son are in the father's workshop sifting through old photographs, blowing off the dust and trying to recognize past people and places.

"In his late eighties at the time of shooting," Malas told me that day, "Shahbandar was almost blind. But he's refusing a cataract operation because the light on which he now depends is in his head." Like Beethoven he did not let the loss of his key sense deter him.

In the last scene of Malas' *Chiaroscuro* Shahbandar gets into bed fully clothed and turns off the light. We are left with a black screen that represents the darkness of neglect that shrouds the memory of this great man. But also of the man who made this film. Although Shahbandar's role in pioneering Arab cinema should have been considered reason for national pride, he has never been recognized and the government would not permit Malas' *Chiaroscuro* to be screened. The only time it was shown in Syria was in 1993 at the American Cultural Center in Damascus.

After the credits I left the sitting room unusually moved by this story. I thought of my father, a gentle, disappointed man who had died three years earlier. I stood in the kitchen of the tiny apartment trying to collect myself, when his wife joined me:

"Miriam, this is about Muhammad, you know. This is how he sees his life and legacy."

It was through the obscured life of this arch national figure that Malas may have been writing his own story: "My story with film," he told Porteus, "is a story of lost love, a love that has deserted, fled. This is what drives me, for we all revere and search for those things we have lost" (Porteous 1995, 210).

Feature films and documentaries honored abroad and ignored at home, virtual house arrest and daily uncertainty about what was permitted and what forbidden; this is the Kafkaesque world in which Malas and other filmmakers functioned in 1980s and 1990s Syria.

Politically daring films were commissioned only to remain unfinished due to lack of funding, or, once completed, they might simply disappear.

The National Film Organization did not ban films, but it might refuse to show them: "Because there's something wrong with the tape. It will be screened when we find someone to repair it. Not just anyone; we need a specialist." And the repair could take years. Even directors were not allowed to have their own copies of their films, or if they did, they were copies of copies of copies. The tape of *City Dreams* that Malas and I were using was in such bad shape that I could not make out many of the details in most of the scenes. And he did not even own a poor copy of *Night*.

Non-Syrian critics have expressed surprise and confusion at this paradoxical situation, not understanding why a state would sponsor a film it does not plan to screen or even release (Porteous 1995, 209; Kennedy-Day 2001, 365, 396).[13] And this paradox is incomprehensible without an understanding of the ways state-sponsored filmmaking functions in authoritarian regimes. More than most cultural products in Hafiz Asad's Syria, films played an important role in commissioned criticism. The Ministry of Culture could commission a film that would be known to be critical of the system and even of the leader. The NFO would be aware of every aspect of the film, from treatment to the final cut; it would pass on all the stages and then refuse to release it.

The key for potential Syrian audiences was not the film itself, in other words, its availability for screening. It was enough to know that filmmakers like Malas had been commissioned to make a film. His reputation guaranteed that the film would venture into forbidden territory. The mere fact that such a film was being made was more important than actually seeing it, since everyone knew that these films were unlikely to be screened in Syria.

These state-sponsored films were kept in Syria to be shown on special occasions when a display of freedom and democracy seemed necessary or warranted. When tensions ran high, films could be shown to an audience desperate for an occasion to share with others their sense of oppression and constant surveillance, and their relief that someone had been brave enough to articulate resistance. Although their films were scarcely, if ever, shown to the public for whom they were made, filmmakers in 1990s Syria played a critical role in providing a context for a communal experience and expression of dissent.

What are we to make of these difficult films that function as political critique and forum for release of pent-up anger even as they run the risk of enabling the injustice to persist? Acclaimed abroad and banned at home, they garnered both aesthetic and political kudos even while the conditions of their production were so uncertain.

In 1994, ten years after its production and time enough to establish its reputation as a classic, *City Dreams* was included on a list of the ten best Arab films ever made. However, when the Ministry of Information disseminated the news about the list it omitted *City Dreams* without explaining why only nine names were published. There was only one Syrian film on the top-ten list, and the Syrian government refused to acknowledge it. Malas might well have seen his own future reflected in Shahbandar's past.

"So what is your next film?" I asked him the last time we met.

"*On the Sand under the Sun*, the story by Ghassan al-Jaba'i."

For my prison cell is my body
And the ode incidental freedom . . .
But I, when a woman falls heavily
At the end of night, I forget my hands
On her voice, and then she slips away
Leaving me my chains,
To write something, finally
Give me back a little space
Since my cell is a body I claim
And a freedom that claims me
—FARAJ BAIRAQDAR,
"Neighing"

chapter seven

LIGHTEN YOUR STEP

Ghassan al-Jaba'i opened his book of plays and read me the epigraph
to the last one, entitled *Bodi the Guard*: "Lighten your step for I believe that the skin of the earth is made up of these bodies" (1995,
103).

I was puzzled. Why had he used this line from the eleventh-century
Syrian poet Abu al-'Ala al-Ma'arri? And why was he quoting it immediately upon meeting me?

"When you return to Mezze this afternoon, pay attention to the
stretch of road between the University and the Customs."

"Why?" I whispered.

"Ten meters below the tarmac of the Mezze Autostrade is the prison where I spent the last of my ten years inside. Some time in 1992, they blindfolded me and took me out of Sadnaya. We drove a while and then I was led down thirty-three steps to a world cut off from air and natural light. For a year, I saw only by electric light and breathed only recycled air. Most people walking on the Autostrade, and who have grown accustomed to this life and, therefore, prefer not to think, would not believe me. If you were to ask anyone walking the Mezze Ustrad whether they knew they were walking on the heads of men imprisoned for doing nothing but thinking wrong thoughts, they would not believe you."

Ghassan al-Jaba'i had been "out" for four years but his handsome face was ravaged, the eyes dull and sad, the skin yellowed.

On my way home, I did more than just pay attention. I got out of the microtaxi at the University stop, and then walked the mile that covered the underground prison. It is the only deserted part of the Autostrade and I felt conspicuous. I shuddered with dread to think that every day, in and out of the city, I was driving over the bodies of hundreds of men cramped into tiny, airless spaces, some with the prospect of eking out the rest of their lives in this terrible place. I noticed nothing untoward and was struck again by the ability of the system to hide its horrors.

This Mezze underground prison was where al-Jaba'i placed Bodi the Guard in his windowless hut surrounded by devils and the souls of the murdered waiting to be born (1995, 120). In the play, this multitude is caged in with wooden pillars and beams that look like a dark forest, like a prison of bars. Bodi's hut in the middle of a prison yard is both above and below ground, both panopticon and solitary cell, and Bodi with his amputated leg (amputated by whom and why?) is both jailor and prisoner, both torturer and the one being tortured. Bodi is obsessed with the footsteps, the millions of footsteps, the lifetime of footsteps that come between him and his birth (his release?).

So, lighten your step!

"Life is sighs and moans. Footsteps. Heartbeats" (al-Jaba'i 1995,

110–111). Bodi lives among underground men whose "prone bodies support the forest, their eyes staring up" (113).

Bodi's haunted hut somewhere below the surface of the earth recalls Marie Seurat's description of her Damascus neighborhood, where the night was filled with "the howls rising out of the basement of a printing press close-by where the information agency, the infamous *mukhabarat*, had set up shop" (1988, 99). These are the twentieth-century *oubliettes*,[1] what Hannah Arendt calls the "veritable holes of oblivion into which people stumble by accident and without leaving behind them such ordinary traces of former existence as a body or a grave" (1979, 434). Looking at the deserted stretch of road between the University and the Customs, I wondered how many buildings sat atop such torture chambers.

We had met with surprising ease. Ghassan al-Jaba'i was teaching at the Institute for Theatrical Studies, close to the Asad Library. When he was first released he was not allowed to teach, because Article 63 of the Syrian Penal Code forbids ex-convicts from teaching for at least ten years (HRW/ME 1995, vol. 7, no. 4). In 1996 the prohibition on teaching was revoked, and the government commissioned him to write a television series.

With some trepidation I phoned him, expecting not to find him, or, if I did, to be put off. Yet he suggested quite simply that I should come over right away. We could meet before six in the Institute cafeteria. It was late afternoon, and the place was empty, the floor strewn with the leftovers of earlier meals and meetings.

When I caught sight of him I felt suddenly shy. I was not sure where to begin. How could I ask him about the stories that evoked his time inside? Did he know that I knew that he had spent ten years in prison? Would my questions about the meanings of opaque allusions and surreal passages seem stupid or prying?

But he was surprisingly relaxed and matter-of-fact, if always guarded, never raising his voice much above a whisper. He was delighted that I had read and liked his 1994 short story collection, *Banana Fingers*. But he was curious also.

"How did you find out about it?"

"Muhammad Malas recommended it to me a few months ago."

Ibrahim Samu'il

I met Samu'il in June 1996 at the French Institute. He was hanging out with Malas and the chair of my lecture on "Culture Is Humanity's Highest Need." He was immediately drawn to my project. A progressive nationalist and a Greek Orthodox, he had spent the four years between 1977 and 1981 inside. He was released a year before the purge of Muslim Brothers in Hama which increased the numbers of prisoners and worsened their treatment. Between 1985 and 1992, he had worked as a counselor in a juvenile correction facility in Qidsiya, near Damascus.

"Why did you choose to return to prison?" I asked, one evening when he invited me to have dinner with him and his wife.

"I wanted to know these kids. I wanted to know all about their families and how they had been brought up." Samu'il had a bachelor's degree in psychology. "Sometimes they would be put into this facility because of a little mistake. One boy was there because of an accident: he had poked a stick in another boy's eye. I wanted them to feel free, so I let them go home, even though, obviously, this was not allowed. I didn't want them to learn real crimes in this school of crimes. As you know, for all of us the line between committing and not committing crimes is sometimes no wider than a hair."

Samu'il had been held in the other Mezze prison, the one up on the hill overlooking Damascus, not the underground prison where Ghassan had spent his last year. In fact, he seemed to think that there was no such prison, confirming Ghassan's assumption that people don't know about the prison unless they have actually been there.

"Prison," Samu'il told me, "can be a key to creativity, but it can also be a trap. It was so hard to write these stories. I kept asking myself, what did I have to add to all the prison literature that is already out there? How could I write without exaggeration, without needing to convince the reader of the evil I had experienced? How could I prevent politics from interfering with art? Writing, especially this kind of writing, is like extracting oil out of the soil and then purifying it. It is the search for the line, what I call the *barzakh*, that both separates but also brings together the explicit and the hidden.[2] It is the breath that makes one person a writer and the other a cook. My challenge to myself was to convey the absolute simultaneity of life and death that is part of the prison experience. It's like being in boiling and freezing water at the same instant. How could I show the way dreams persist even when everything else has stopped? What I learned was that no one can stop thoughts and dreams. I still dream. Maybe I'm Don Quixote, that crazy guy who couldn't stop dreaming. Or maybe it's impossible to eliminate resistance whatever form it takes because it is a law of nature."

When we met he talked about the fear of prison and how "they" came in the night, "that is their time, so that if you think that you can use the cover of darkness to hide, you're wrong. They dragged me out of bed where I was lying next to Marmush." He looked affectionately at the large comfortable woman who was busy preparing dinner in their sparse kitchen. For the next eight months they did not see each other.

"I kept trying to find out where Ibrahim was. I went to what I discovered was an interrogation center and one day I heard someone use a password that gained him entry. The next day, I used the word I'd heard and I got in." Marmush chuckled aloud at the memory. "Then I met the director and I pretended to be very naïve. I told him that Ibrahim and I had just married and that I needed his advice. Should I stay with this man? What was his crime? If it was rape or theft or murder, shouldn't I divorce him? He said that his crime was politics, and I said that's impossible because I've never seen him on TV. The director was getting annoyed and he asked me: What's television got to do with anything? And so I said: Everyone knows that all politicals are on TV."

They burst out laughing. Despite his exasperation, the director had believed her. That was how she learned where Ibrahim was and could visit him occasionally.

Dedicated to Marmush, many of Samu'il's stories figure women who share their men's horror while waiting or attending clandestine meetings or being awoken at midnight by the dreaded knock on the door. In the black of night a couple clutch at each other, alert to every little telltale sound. The raindrops pinging on the tin roof punctuate their terror-ridden embrace, trusting that touch, smell, and sound will stand in for sight. The car door slamming at the end of the alley sends the fugitive flying out of the house, and she slips back into bed where "loneliness ate her body" (Samu'il 1990, 21).

Samu'il spent one hundred days in isolation. He could tell the passage of time because of the meals he received. Those were the worst of times and they remained engraved on his mind. During the more than three years that he was inside he wrote stories in his head. He did not want to write them down, even though he did have paper smuggled in, lest they lose the freshness of what he called the "flash." Nine years later he wrote about the wrenching transformations undergone by the prisoners: "I look over sixty. I know," he said when I had been unable to conceal my surprise that he was only forty-five. He wrote about children who rejected their father when he finally returned after years inside. The children often preferred photographs and stories to their broken reality.

Some prisoners were not allowed visits for years on end and they would continue to visualize a world that was in the process of disappearing. In his essay about Syrian prisons, critic Mohammed Atassi writes, "Many prisoners started their jail term young and energetic, and left a remnant of a person. When some found their homes the key would not work in the door. When the released prisoner eventually found his family, he discovered that they had been waiting for him for twenty years; they did not live their lives—no marriage, no divorce, no celebration. Yet, they could not easily recognize his face." But, of course, time also changed those outside who had waited so long. Faraj Bairaqdar tells the sad story of a prisoner who had his first visit after ten years inside. He saw what he thought were his parents weeping and he asked his mother why, "but the woman cried even harder, 'I am your sister, your mother is dead'" (Atassi 2004, 6, 11).

The title story of *Light Coughs* (Samu'il 1990) evokes the loneliness of the one inside. After long lying alone in his tiny cell, a prisoner realizes that he can communicate with the next cell. He does so by clearing his throat. When his neighbor responds the cell expands around him. Their antiphonal coughs twist a "rope of light coughs" that illumines the darkness (52). They continue their correspondence while the guard is at a distance. Then, one day when the prisoner pulls the nail out of the wooden cell door in order to peek out through its tiny hole, he sees the guard. The neighbor clears his throat. He does not respond. His neighbor coughs again and again, each time louder. Suddenly, the guard bursts into the neighbor's cell and all he can hear is the echo of flesh on flesh and then silence, and then "like a snail retreating into its darkness the beam of light withdrew from my cell and its walls closed in on my cold, cold body" (54). These light coughs return in other stories. They are the language without words that allows prisoners to hold on to their humanity. Its meaning cannot be fixed but this language is the only remaining thing that belongs to the one clearing his throat.

Just before being released Samu'il was asked whether he had any requests. He clearly relished rehearsing his admonition to the prison director: "'I would urge you to think about the prisoners as animals and to accord them equal rights.' The director asked me to explain so I suggested that he squeeze as many cows as he could into our twelve-by-ten-meters cell. Then he should count the cows and however many they were that would be the maximum number of prisoners for that cell." He was savoring that moment. He went on quoting himself: "Oh, by the way, the food is not fit for dogs. Test it. Put a bowl of our food in front of a dog and see if he'll eat it. If he does, this food is fit for the prisoners. If he doesn't, then don't!" He had written of such food in *Stench*, where the stink of the lunch is such that the prisoner cannot touch the tomato and cauliflower mess despite his hunger that "spread across the space of the cramped cell to await the next day's midday hour" (1990, 68).

He continued with his parting speech to the prison director: "Don't make eighty men share one toilet so that those in the back of the line have to do their business in their pants."

"I can't believe you were released after that speech."

"Yes, you're right. He understood. The last thing he said was: You're the most dangerous of all. If you talk like this about food and sleep, what might you say about politics!"

But release did not bring freedom. Ibrahim told me what I was to hear again on my last day in Syria: prison life is not much more oppressive than life on the outside. "Prison is tattooed on my soul so that it flows in the blood of all that I write. The beatings may go but the pain in the soul lasts forever. I will always crave light and love. I will never be free of the fear to be locked up again without knowing why, and without recourse to a lawyer, a judge, or a trial. With a sentence you can at least check the days off the calendar. Under martial law, when you have no right to a lawyer, a judge, a trial, or a sentence, you live in limbo. Life outside is no different from inside; there is no end in sight. I feel like a man wandering around the desert with a helicopter hovering overhead."

This is the violence grown ordinary of surveillance by foe, friend, and family. In the title story of *The Stench of Heavy Steps* (1988) a woman is told to meet her fugitive husband in a street. But if she senses danger when he approaches, she must just walk on. Hearing heavy steps behind her she walks past the man for whom she has longed for two years, overcome by the stench of the steps behind her. When she has shaken the steps, she returns to the rendezvous. He has disappeared and so she returns to the daily bread of waiting without hope of reprieve. Like other prisoners' wives she will wait engulfed in the void of his absence.

The absence of political prisoners is "sordid, suspended, killing, [tasting] of bitter despair, a despair that creeps like cancer into the lost hopes of family members, between the possible and the impossible" (Atassi 2004, 6). Inside, the prospect of meeting with loved ones fills the prisoner with joy, dread, and anxiety in equal measure. The thought of these rare and precious visits becomes an overwhelming preoccupation, and it dominates the prisoners' imaginary. During their months, and sometimes years, of waiting prisoners and their families prepare for the brief encounter between two individuals from two different realms. They create a fiction with which they hope to identify.

In his 28 January 2005 interview with Fadil al-Fadil, the poet Faraj Bairaqdar recalls his own contradictory feelings before each visit; he was at once fearful and exhilarated. The most wonderful visitors, the angels, were the women who allowed him briefly "to leave his hell for paradise." Whenever the jailor announced a visit he would try to organize his thoughts and write down everything he had on his mind. But then, when he returned to the cell and looked at his notes, he realized that he had not even touched on any of the topics. And so he would add more thoughts and questions for the next time, only to experience the same failure all over again. But each time it was worse because there were more thoughts and more questions than the last time. Some of the prisoners returned from such visits elated and others deeply depressed. He described his own roller-coaster emotions:

At the beginning of the visit I sometimes felt that the skies were bending down and God was smiling. At other times the visit was a wounding awakening that confirmed the distance and the depth of my absence. . . . When I returned I was exhausted and needed to sleep or weep alone. But with the passage of the years, I trained myself to apathy immediately after the visit. . . . Some of the prisoners prepare themselves for the visits like a child getting ready for a party. They put on new clothes and from early morning they look out of the high windows. As soon as they catch sight of the visitors they start to wave and shout even though they know that they are putting their visit at risk. (al-Fadil 2005)

It is this part of the visit that Samu'il described in "The Toilet." Although the prisoner knows that his family cannot get beyond the prison gate and that he cannot get closer than the very high window above the communal toilet, he splashes on perfume, dresses, and pulls himself up to the toilet window (1990, 79–92). Squeezing his arms through the bars, he stretches down to the figures in the distance. Samu'il drew for me a picture that he called "*masafat al-shawq,* the distance of longing, the gap where dreams are broken." Written from the vantage point of several years outside, Samu'il had the distance to laugh a little.

I recalled Mamduh 'Adwan's words, "Ibrahim draws us into the prison or into the atmosphere created by fear of the prison. Once there he compels us to recognize the similarity between official confinement and the suffocating constraints of our daily lives. Our life is hell."

These were the words he wrote in his introduction to Samu'il 's Stench. 'Adwan had criticized those who use prison literature to lionize the individual who has been inside, especially the one who presents in excruciating detail the torture he has undergone. Such testimonial writing, he believed, compromises the poetry of prison writing that is so essential to convey the meaning of the experience. Mamduh praised Samu'il for his refusal to write politically.

"This kind of literature," 'Adwan wrote in his introduction, "reminds us of our lost humanity, our humanity that is found in our little relationships, our little pains and concerns, our little dreams. . . . After I read this collection my sensitivity to danger and fear increased. That is the Cause" (Samu'il 1988, 13).

Ghassan al-Jaba'i

Ghassan al-Jaba'i was a different story altogether. Unlike Samu'il 's linear narrative of dread, capture, and release with a good dose of black humor, al-Jaba'i's story was halting and choked. The memories were still too raw to be tractable.

Ghassan was a Shubati who spent his first four years in Tadmur, the next four in Sadnaya, and the last under the Mezze Autostrade. He had been released as part of the general amnesty following the 1991 Madrid Conference on peace in the Middle East. He commented cynically that the real reason for his release was not a new sensitivity to human rights but the need for more cells. After the 1991 Gulf War, the government cracked down on those who had sympathized with Saddam Hussein.

So who had published these stories and plays that had been written while al-Jaba'i was in jail? I had searched everywhere for my own copy of *Banana Fingers* and could not find it. Damascus bookstore keepers had not even heard of it. Yet, the Ministry of Culture had published it and Shawqi Baghdadi (b. 1928), an established writer, had written the introduction. Everywhere I was greeted with blank looks. Finally I went to the Ministry for a copy. While a clerk was fetching the book from the warehouse, 'Ali al-Qayyim, the deputy minister, wanted to know how I had found out about *Banana Fingers*. I felt like a spy caught in the act, even though all I wanted was a book the Ministry had published.

The introduction is intriguing in the way it acknowledges the artistry of the writing while taking Shawqi Baghdadi off the hook. Adopting a distant tone, he claims that he had never heard of al-Jaba'i. He writes well, but some of the stories are too long. The only hint that these stories are about prison is the statement that the author "had been forced to distance himself from the world for ten whole years. No sooner had he returned than his name began to be spread around as the writer of stories and plays whose vitality had not been dampened by his long break from humanity." He closes patronizingly: "He might not have been vouchsafed the deep and intense conversations about human existence with companions inside had he remained in ordinary life" (al-Jaba'i 1994, 8–9). Ah, the aesthetic advantages of confinement!

A government intellectual and the Ministry of Culture had officially sanctioned a piece of prison literature. The obvious assumption is that a government that itself publishes literature critical of its treatment of its people must be democratic and a champion of human rights. Or not. Here was another example of commissioned criticism, whose publication, paradoxically, had to be connected with the government that had the prerogative to control its distribution. In this case, however, it seemed to matter less whether the publication of the book made the government look good. It was more about a game the state, or at least certain members of the state apparatus, were playing with the dissident.

Ghassan told me that the Ministry of Culture had expressed concern about the identification of the prison with the location of his writing, so they did not permit him to include the names Tadmur or Sadnaya or Mezze at the end of each story.[3] But they did indicate the dates of writing. Two years later, they published three of his four plays written inside: *Generalius*, *Sister*, and *Bodi the Guard*. The Ministry of Culture refused to include *The Ghoul*, claiming that the depiction of the governor of the Tadmur prison was too obvious.

Ghassan gave me the banned manuscripts of *The Ghoul* and a short story titled "A Syrian Green Card: Confessions of a Little Man." Struck by the convention of using *ghoul* as a title, I read *The Ghoul* for the forbidden that I assumed it must contain and, to my surprise, found the play innocuous. The few jabs at a patriarchal figure seemed less daring than much of what he had written in the other plays and in the stories. Why had this play been censored? What were the criteria for censorship? Had I missed some dangerous references because I did not have the key? Or was this just a lesson in the arbitrariness of power and the production of Foucault's docile bodies?

The Wednesday after our meeting in the cafeteria of the Institute for Theatrical Studies, Ghassan came for lunch with his wife and two children, their ages separated by the length of his time inside. Until I heard the bell ring, I had doubted he would come. Once the introductory formalities were over and the children were running around the courtyard fountain, he started to speak. The sunlight shimmered through the grape trellis, yet he retained the look of a man trapped in the dark.

Upon his return in 1981 from six years of graduate study at the Kiev School of Drama, he had been conscripted into the army. Almost immediately he was disappeared. For eighteen months, the only reply his wife ever received to her constant questions about his whereabouts was that she should stop thinking about him. One day, the wife of a prisoner with al-Jabaʿi told her to get a visitor's permit. She was to go to the "desert," that is, Tadmur. Taking their little boy, she made the 130-kilometer trip. She smiled when she recalled how astonished Ghassan had been that Umar was so big.

"Is that our son?!" They scarcely spoke. Not then and not even later. Only in writing could he express the hell he had experienced.

What troubled him most was the overcrowding. Particularly after Hama, the cells were so overcrowded that—with only two meters by forty centimeters per person—the men had to sleep on their sides to fit. Cells for ten were crowded with up to seventy men.[4] His stories evoke the mood inside without direct description: animals of all kinds and the relentless dark and fear of death. He developed linguistic and formal strategies to evade censorship. He was using a version of the Russian Aesopian language that might be termed *lugha muqaffaʿiya*, or Muqaffaian language, a term I derive from Ibn al-Muqaffaʿ, the famed ninth-century writer of animal fables.[5] Al-JabaʿI's hyenas, birds, and spiders take the reader into torture chambers and underground solitary confinement.

For a few moments every day the men walked around the perimeter of what is called the *sahat al-tanaffus*, literally, "the breathing yard," "a square of light fenced in by spiders' legs, fenced in by fear" (al-Jabaʿi 1994, 200, 87). The yards were the lungs of the prison, but sometimes they were filled with blood. The prisoners were sent out so that the sun might burn off the bugs nested in their hair and clothes. With time, Ghassan refused to go for fear of his return to the dark of the cell. But it was not only the dread of the return to the cell that made the sahat al-tanaffus a place of horror. It was there that the previous night's victims were hanged. The prisoners would enter the yard, "an army of black skeletons crawling over the earth of the naked, cement yard, an intertwined, interwoven army like the string of pigeons *hanged* [*mashnuq*] from the hunter's waist. . . . A school of sardines goes out daily to dry on the sand, under the burning, desert sun." On the walls are "thick drops of oil" which soon disappear (87).

"That," Ghassan explained, "was how the shadows of the hanging cadavers appeared on the walls."

He had underlined the word "hanged" (mashnuq) in the book he had dedicated to me. This word was the only clue he gave the reader as to what the oil stains might be. There might be one oil stain/shadow, or two or three, and then they would disappear. The spectacle was a warning, a daily lesson.[6]

Birds of all kinds hovered over the square. Some fledglings "with their ashen wings and waxen beaks" were preparing to take their maiden flight when "one of them fell into the square roofed in with barbed wire. Before it could reach the edge of the opposite wall the sparrow hawks in their high leather boots and cocked red berets swooped down. They loaded their automatic rifles and competed to decapitate the baby bird" (90). Briefly, the boots, berets, and automatic rifles take the description out of the metaphorical. Almost immediately, however, we return to the mother bird that lost her young to the sparrow hawks. In her house decorated with branches of palm and basil she "slaughtered for him the biggest cock she had and when she saw no blood she was sure he would return. But the years passed" (91). Animal tenderness rubs up against human violence, and each pigeon/sardine/prisoner chained to his two neighbors knows that tomorrow his may be the thick drop of oil on the wall.

"Even though we weren't allowed to write," Ghassan told me, "I got hold of paper and pen. I had to write to survive. When they want to eliminate you, you have to assert your existence. You write to live! But I don't write politically, directly. I write critical realism. This is a form of politics because I am addressing the human condition." Unlike Ibrahim Samu'il, he had to write while inside.

Faraj Bairaqdar confirmed the existential importance of writing inside. Poetry offered a way to "control my prison rather than be controlled by it. . . . Love is one of the ingredients of resistance. Poetry. Despair also, but not in a suicidal or capitulatory sense. . . . Two weeks after my imprisonment began, poetry came by itself, as a defense mechanism" (Atassi 2004, 9). In Tadmur writing was absolutely forbidden, and so during their four and five years there both al-Jaba'i and Bairaqdar memorized their stories and poetry and were able to transcribe them only when they were moved to Sadnaya.

"I used to believe in the power of culture to intervene politically and to make a difference," al-Jaba'i said. "But with time, I realized that all that mattered was to write truthfully. Literature has its effects whatever the author's intention. It is crucial not to be explicit but to experiment. The surreal and the hallucinatory become the basic elements of a new kind of writing in which the unconscious becomes the hero."

The unconscious organizes the chaos of allusions and gives them meaning. In the intensity of light and heat there is a forced silence, he once wrote, that turns human beings into echoes, "deep croaks of a drop of water in the bottom of a well ... oww ... owww ..." (al-Jaba'i 1994, 88). Each human became the sound of pain echoing throughout the building in the dead of the night. And those whose pain was the loudest were the Muslim Brothers, the Hama survivors.

"I must've missed that. Where did you write about the Brothers?"

"Remember the section where I wrote: 'Can we forget the sound?' I said: 'Sound [sawt] or whip [sawt]?'" (88).

Yes, I had had no idea what the homonyms meant. The sound of the whip, Ghassan said, was often accompanied by another sound, the sound of the Muslim Brothers' voices screaming: "Allahu akbar! God is great!" No matter how much they were tortured, the Muslim Brothers, or at least those whom Ghassan heard, continued to praise God. I remembered the reports of the June 1980 massacre of hundreds of Muslim Brothers in their Tadmur cells that echoed "to the fearful din of automatic weapons, exploding grenades, and dying shrieks of 'God is great!'" (Seale 1989, 329). No one in Syria was writing about the Muslim Brothers, especially not about their torture. They were supposed to have been eliminated and forgotten. Yet their grisly night screams affirmed that they had not been eliminated. However indirectly, Ghassan memorialized the suffering but also the steadfastness of fellow inmates.

In his play Sister, a Palestinian demented by torture utters a monologue that only once and briefly presents his nightly experience of being beaten and silenced while they whip him, beat the soles of his feet, pluck out his mustache hair by hair, crush his teeth, beat his head with their shoes, rifle butts, the table, and the walls, and "before dawn, my brothers, they sealed my window with reinforced concrete. Laughing sarcastically. The guards are so afraid. Why are they afraid? Whom do they fear? They don't want the windows to hear my screams or to see them. They don't want the sun to see them" (al-Jaba'i 1995, 77).

On Fridays in Sadnaya, the least grim of the three prisons in which al-Jaba'i was held, the prisoners met in the common area beyond the cells to read literature, listen to political lectures, or watch someone's play. During these sessions, which might last as long as six hours, Ghassan had directed plays, some of which he had written, including *Generalius*, a play about a tyrannical ruler. It is the only piece of al-Jaba'i's writings that has not only the date, 1988, but also the place, Sadnaya. Like Mamduh 'Adwan's *The Ghoul*, it directly targeted the Asad cult. This transparently political farce about Caesar and his people must have delighted the inmates. They must have loved the soothsayer who warns the great leader that if he takes off his clothes he will become a generalius. Does generalius mean naked? (See figure 11 for a clay representation of the mockery of such notions of democracy.) But when Caesar asks him what he means, he admits that he does not know what a generalius is but he'd read the word in the papers. So Caesar orders him to be wrapped in newspaper and left on the ground, a warning to those who threaten their leaders with words they have taken from the media.

In another scene some try on gas masks, but Caesar forbids their use except "for prisoners" because they prevent one from speaking (1995, 17). Safety lies in silence. But this is also the new democracy, where prisoners are protected from chemical weapons in order to silence them, and the leader exposes himself to danger so that he can keep on speaking. The leader elaborates the democratic message by telling his people not to kneel to him any more. They should just stand. Forever.

The crowds are then given carnival masks that accord with their professions. The Executioner warns a poet not to wear his lest Caesar recognize him, and "kick your head and say to you: I don't want to see your face after today or I'll have you arrested. Go away!" (22). Scenes of celebration are undercut by chants:

We decorate the streets at his command
We decorate the air
We carry images
We carry men
We extinguish the moon
We starve, wretched and naked

"The Citizens' Right to Be Elected." In Abbas and Maala, *Citizenship Guide* (2005), p. 46.

We die a thousand times over

But Rome survives; Caesar's Rome; Rome's Caesar; at his command.

(27)

Unlike the drugged citizens that Vaclav Havel criticized for their as-if behavior, these citizens shout out their awareness. They are not plastering the walls of the city with the tyrant's images out of love but out of fear or because they have been ordered to do so. Told to cheer the leader, they obey because their life depends on their obedience to Caesar, whose power is everywhere. Then comes the real leader from the people, Brutus, and he kills the tyrant. Unlike Wannus's Zakariya in *The Elephant, Oh King of Ages*, who crumbles in the presence of the king, Brutus retains the strength of his convictions because he is supported by the people. At his trial, Brutus Ibn 'Abdallah denies having killed Caesar; the man he had tried to kill for love of Rome was not Caesar but the Dictator, and he had not died (37). Echoing 'Adwan's Chorus, 'Abdallah proclaims that it is not enough to kill the tyrant for tyranny to end. Then the play enters a time warp: "I killed no one. Caesar is not my father. Caesar lived 2,000 years ago. I have come across him in books only. My father was an army sergeant killed in 1967" (52). Reference to the year 1967 and the Six Days' War returns us to Malas' *Night* and his questioning of the collusion between the Israelis and the Syrian military in the destruction of Kuneitra in the Golan.

"What was your crime?" I felt comfortable enough by the end of the afternoon in the garden of my Mezze apartment to ask him directly.

"I don't know exactly. I don't know who betrayed me. None of us did. These questions obsessed us political prisoners."

"To whom shall I point the finger of blame?" a prisoner exclaims. "To the night? OK. I'll accuse the night that left its color on our stones" (al-Jaba'i 1994, 169–170). The atmosphere is so thick with suspicion and fear that the only reasonable object of accusation is the night under whose dark cover so much evil is committed. Those responsible are the night, the tyrannical government, other people, but also the individual himself because "when you point one finger at someone, you need to know that your three other fingers are point-ing at you" (173). But who are you? "I am a cause without a goal" (183).

"The reasons for our being inside were Kafkaesque, unfathom-able," he said. "Many of us were imprisoned for our intention to turn our unrealized desires into forbidden dreams. Yes, it is dangerous to dream here."

Here again were those dangerous dreams, dangerous because they led to belief in another kind of world and then to sacrifice on its be-half. But they were dangerous also because, like the sahat al-tanaffus, the breathing yard, they make the return to reality so unbearable.

Chasing dreams like butterflies leads to jail (169). But dreams do not die inside, only outside, so that when the prisoner comes out and the world is transformed his dreams dissipate: "They had left a gap-ing hole in the memory. . . . So what was the point of recording those generations of dreaming. . . . Is it possible that all we dreamt was completely empty?" (174, 211). This is the realization of those outside: the dreams inside were just that, dreams.

The one story al-Jaba'i asked me to read was "The Gallows," written in 1989, probably in Sadnaya: "You'll like it because it's about some-one like you who is interested in what we have experienced. So our experiences are put in a museum."

I feared that I might not quite like the person he thought I was. I opened the book.

The sun spreads its crystalline fingers. The dust comes to life and you discover for the second time that the void is full. . . . Billions and billions of tiny particles blow around in chaotic, bewildering liveliness toward the rectangle stained with colors, no one knows how or when they were mixed and plastered on top of each other. . . . The first thing to appear on the wall opposite the windows are tiny circles of light—none larger than a goldpiece—pressed together, interweaving, piled on top of each other like a mound of washed oranges in a muddy yard. . . . Transparent tubes spray the dust—no doubt piercing the opposite wall and passing through it to somewhere out there. . . . Some said they were spears of light that now and again penetrate the space so that these delicate creatures should not decompose and the place should not suffocate. This is true. . . . Others were sure they were prison bars. . . . Existential bars through which darkness passes, and people copied them and made them out of steel so that light might pass. This also is true. (al-Jaba'i 1994, 97–98)

The ambiguity of light tubes and prison bars recalls the lovers' conversation about wires and bars in *The Extras*. In this story, the exquisite delicacy of the sun's first light turns the empty cell into a circus of movement and colors. The light is first seen as crystalline fingers and then transparent tubes able to pass through walls and then spears and finally prison bars. These are the bars through which the light must pass and which absorb the light into themselves. Is this really the sun? The hint of light is seen, felt, smelled, and almost tasted in the freshly washed citrus. The prisoners' voices jumble together, each seeing the sun in the uncanny light.

The only way to find the source of the light is to have someone look directly at it. He would have to be lifted high to the window to check whether the light came from the sun, the moon, or the street lamps. The prisoners make a human pyramid, and a thin blond man jumps to the top, grabs hold of the bars, and looks out. What he sees so shocks him that he remains frozen, stuck to the bars, even after the human pyramid collapses beneath him.

"He had become *mashnuq al-daw'*," Ghassan told me over lunch. "He was hanged by the light. Once he had seen what was outside the hell of the cell, he could not go back. The vision killed him."

There again was the "hanging" metaphor. The blond prisoner was hanged on a rope of light, with his chin still on the windowsill and his body "flowing" over the wall (105). This image recalls the dark oil stains on the sahat al-tanaffus wall, the shadows of the men hanged the previous night in the yard where the prisoners will walk the next morning. An abrupt transition takes us to a museum where the hanged man is on view, and a female tourist asks her guide why they do not cover the skull with some hair. The guide promises to convey her recommendation to the museum director. The cadaver is kept for posterity, and for foreigners.

These stories read visually, like dark, unframed oil paintings. At most, there is some white to offset the unremitting black: dark cells, Sweida (the Roman town in the south built out of black rock), the ink, the night, and then the snow and the occasional lights, like an Escher print with one hallucination fitting into the negative of another. A man grown delirious in confinement applies coats of black paint to the dirty white walls of a basement that turns into a cave where skeletons were

> the only white things in this black chasm. Two skeletons sitting at a skeleton table . . . drinking wine out of two small skulls and behind them the sea . . . a black sea. . . . The coast was black . . . the sky was black. . . . On the roof was a child's skeleton in its mother's belly, its head was bigger than its body, curled around itself as though to kiss his buttocks. The umbilical cord disappears in the blackness and above him hovers another skeleton like it but with wings, wings of bone and a black halo surrounds them. It was only above the door that he had left a square of white with a black dove in the center lying in a nest like a diaphragm with snakes beneath its wings. It disappeared . . . became a myth. (139)

Here is the realm of mythical beings reduced to the tight airlessness of prison, where men gasp for life as they teeter over the edge of the abyss. Each man and his shadow "take refuge from other men in fire" (88). Some seek solace in birds. Far from being symbols of freedom, as might be expected, these birds, with their burned black wings of wax and bone that cradle and shade snakes, are as shackled as the men who see and dream them. Death hangs heavy over these introverted stories.

Before he left that afternoon, Ghassan told me to heed Voltaire: "Standing for one moment in the place of the accused when I am innocent makes me forget a thousand books about freedom I have read." We would talk again, he promised in parting. But there was no next time.

Lessons from a Rogue State

Syrian prison literature provides a prism on life under authoritarian rule, where martial law suspends civil liberties. Any who breathe a word against arbitrary restrictions may disappear. The walls enclosing the mind are sometimes more oppressive than those surrounding the body. Nabil Malih's *The Extras* catches this choking breathlessness in the secret rendezvous of two lovers who cower in fear of they know not what. Terrified by any sound on the stairwell, they dare not talk too loudly lest they be overheard or miss the telltale sound, the stench of heavy steps. The attempt to be alone merely confirms the impossibility of ever being really alone, of ever being able to breathe freely. In stories, plays, and films, ordinary people, police, and informers meld into each other. Danger is always everywhere. It is part of the air that is so hard to breathe, the air that leaves one gasping for air, for tanaffus.

Prison literature articulated the airlessness of life under authoritarian rule. Yet even years inside did not stop some dissidents. After fourteen years inside, Faraj Bairaqdar was released thanks to intervention by the Dutch International Association of Poets. He went to Holland, but he vowed to return even if the state of emergency persists and "there are still prisons, and summons for trials, and depression, and hijacked freedoms" (quoted in Adnan 2004).

To write about Syrian prison literature is not to exceptionalize it, to say that Syrian prisons are much worse than prisons anywhere else. They are not. Throughout the Middle East prisoners have written of conditions not so different from those experienced by Bairaqdar, al-Jaba'i, and Samu'il. Nor does the Middle East own a monopoly on prison literature. The American gulag has produced powerful writings by the system's "undesirables." Black men in the United States enjoy no greater immunity from arbitrary detention than do citizens of the most repressive regimes in the world. In the early 1990s, Bruce Franklin notes, "African Americans were imprisoned at a rate (1,947 per 100,000) six times greater than whites (306 per 100,000) and more than twenty times the international rate of imprisonment (96 per 100,000). . . . The United States, birthplace of the modern prison two centuries earlier, has transformed the prison into a central institution of society, unprecedented in scale and influence" (1998, 17). The history of abuse in U.S. prisons can be read in recent reports about the maltreatment of Iraqi prisoners at Abu Ghraib and of Taliban prisoners at Guantánamo Bay. Investigations revealed that the abuses were systemic, ordered from above, and more or less consistent with domestic practice.

Reflection on the U.S. penal system at home and abroad provides a sobering antidote to self-righteous alarm about Syrian prisons and the society they reflect. The late 'Abd al-Rahman Munif put it well when he wrote that to "discuss the political prison in a confined place such as Iraq or Saudi Arabia, it seems as if I am exonerating other places or as if the political prison does not exist in these places. Yet we know that political prisons exist from the Atlantic to the Gulf to be exact, whether in terms of its environment, means, or concerns" (quoted in Habash 2003, 12).

The anthropologist Susan Slyomovics (2005) has written about the "années de plomb" in Hasan II's Morocco. During these Years of Lead, many political activists were incarcerated, often without habeas corpus, and tortured and sometimes killed. The stories they tell, write, and perform are harrowing and their calls for justice, indemnities, and reparations in the aftermath of Hasan II's death in 1999 are inspiring. In Egypt, where Franklin notes that the 1993 rate of incarceration was only .0062 percent (1998, 16), national literature owes much to political prisoners like Sherif Hetata and Sonallah Ibrahim who were ready to pay the price. Iraqi, Saudi, and Syrian prison literatures are less well known and studied because political conditions have made access to such texts difficult and writing about them tricky.

Why tricky? For an American to write in 2006 about brutal rulers in countries her government is targeting risks justifying outside military intervention. To write about Saddam Hussein's torture chambers could be used to endorse U.S. military intervention to save the Iraqi people. In fact, widespread condemnation of the Iraqi leader's brutality against his people allowed President Bush to save face when he did not find the weapons of mass destruction he had used as pretext to invade Iraq in 2003. When the war could no longer be explained in terms of self-defense, it was turned into a moral mission to rid the world of dictators in order to make it safe for "freedom and democracy."

These two words are not synonymous in the way that their constant twinning would seem to imply. Colorful in his contempt of the Syrian state's sloganeering of "freedom and democracy," Muhammad Maghut's words are instructive for Americans watching their military's actions in the Middle East today: "They gave us parliaments and took our freedom. . . . If a state draws a fluttering dove on the doors of its prisons has it convinced itself and its citizens that there is freedom in the land?" (2001, 234, 258). So the White House draws doves on the doors of its prisons at Guantánamo Bay and Abu Ghraib and calls its designs on Iraq "Operation Enduring Freedom" and "Operation Iraqi Freedom."[7]

chapter eight

LEAVING DAMASCUS

It was my last day in Damascus. I had been longing for this day;
dreading it, too. I didn't know how long I could have gone on without
a good night's sleep, without full lungs, with this persistent sense of
sadness and frustration.

Only a week earlier I couldn't stand the place any longer. I was
out in the pretty garden of our basement apartment; the heat wave
had begun to subside and I should have felt good. We had spent the
morning wandering around Ibn 'Arabi's tomb and visiting the nearby
mosque and madrasa of the eighteenth-century saint 'Abd al-Ghani
al-Nabulsi. Knowing that this might be the last time we would be

there for a while we soaked in the atmosphere. But a little later, while barreling along the stretch of road that is the roof of the Mezze Autostrad prison, I'd had it. We talked about changing our tickets so that we could leave the next day and not have to wait another week. I felt better. So we stayed.

The next morning was cool and clear and we went for a walk with Mamduh 'Adwan. Upon our return home for breakfast the phone rang and interesting people started to fill the coming days with meetings, video screenings, film shoots. The time became short. And before I knew it the last day dawned.

Our first meeting was with Nezam, Bruce's colloquial tutor. During the autumn of 1995, he had come twice a week to our "Louis Farouk" apartment in the fashionable Rawda district. We were two blocks from the U.S. ambassador's residence and three from one of President Hafiz Asad's well-guarded palaces. After quick greetings, they would retire to the balcony facing Mount Qasyun and settle down to a lesson. They would chat animatedly about Wannus's *Historical Miniatures* or a medieval prayer by the thirteenth-century Sufi saint Ibn 'Arabi, and sometimes they watched Lutfi Lutfi's Ramadan miniseries based on Ulfat Idilbi's *Damascus, Smile of Sadness.*

Months passed and we moved into a sweet garden flat in Mezze. Our lives took on a different rhythm, and we rarely saw Nezam. Then in early June he called to invite us to an Arabic adaptation of Kafka's *Metamorphosis* in which he had a small part. On the third day of the show, however, the day we had planned to go, he telephoned, deeply disappointed. The play had been canceled. Financial reasons. He seemed reluctant to pursue the matter on the phone. Whether or not it was true, the fact is the phones felt tapped. Or, as they said in whispers, "The walls have ears." When we ran into each other a few days later, I again asked why the play had been canceled. Again, he did not expand; perhaps some "content problem."

So here we were on our last day, going for the first time to his apartment in the Yarmuk Palestinian refugee camp on the outskirts of Damascus. We picked up the micro, a kind of minibus, on the Mezze Ustrad. For a dime, we traveled for over half an hour in the crowded van that took us from our modern section of Damascus to the poor area of the city that is home to the Palestinian refugee camps.

"Where's the Dair Yassin stop?" I asked one of the passengers, a veiled woman. "Inside."

Sounded like prison.

Two gateways loomed ahead. One led into the Yarmuk camp and the other to the Filastin camp. These camps are not at all the tent cities that we in the West imagine when we hear the words "refugee camps"; the trim buildings and clean streets contrasted with downtown Damascus.

Suddenly the micro screeched to a halt to let on a passenger. It was Nezam.

"Marhaba, hello. I was looking out for you."

Two Americans with hats and sunglasses, squeezed into the back of a ten-passenger van, cannot travel incognito in this area of town where everyone seems to know everyone else. He'd kept a lookout for us, lest we got lost.

Seconds later, we got out at a street corner where an old man was tending his cherry cart. Nezam's place was a few steps further in a building accessed through a metal gate that opened out onto a lovely little courtyard with its characteristic Damascene *bahra*, or fountain. Nezam's room was covered in movie posters and the shelves were lined with books. He immediately offered us food, lots of it and all delicious.

"How is your project? Doctor Bruce tells me that you met al-Jaba'i and Samui'l."

"Yes. Do you know them?"

He looked at me quickly and then whispered, "You know, they have all spent time in prison."

I nodded.

"So have I."

I didn't know what to say.

"We all know each other, those of us who have spent time inside. Anyway, al-Jaba'i is my teacher at the Higher Institute for Theatrical Studies."

He was giving me an opening and I decided to take it: "How long were you in prison?"

"Five years."

"Where were you?"

"Most of the time in Sadnaya, up on the hill. That's where I met Jaba'i. We were in the same wing. He was on the side where the Shubatis were held. I was with the communists even though I wasn't a member. Our cell block backed up on to that of the Shubatis."

He sketched the memory.

"How did you know he was there? How did you meet?"

"We couldn't leave the wing, but we were free to move around the wing once our cell doors were opened around eight in the morning." Lowering his voice, he added, "In fact, we were freer inside than we are here."

Curiously, prisoners in Syria and elsewhere sometimes did indeed know and understand life outside better than those who lived it, because they had extraordinary access to information. Almost anything could be smuggled in, even communist publications. There was an unexpected sense of freedom even under conditions of the greatest

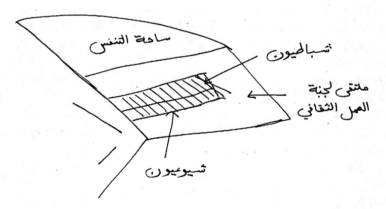

Nezam's sketch of Sadnaya prison wing with its "breathing yard." From top to bottom the names read Breathing yard, Shubatis, Meeting place for the cultural activities committee, communists.

constraint. "I found prison an elating experience," writes the Cuban Jorge Valls, "it was the only 'free territory' in Cuba, the only place where you could say anything you wanted and not be afraid of arrest. Of course, they could still execute you. We were used to the thought of death" (1986, 18). Iranian prison memoirs describe a similar freedom inside: "In the outside world he had always been 'stifled by dogmatism, false ideologies, and self-censorship.' In short, prison was freedom; the outside world was a prison" (Abrahamian 1999, 152). In his autobiography Malcolm X, the Black Muslim leader in 1960s America, reflected on prison education and his excitement at learning so much that was new: "Up to then, I never had been so truly free in my life" (quoted in Franklin 1998, 154). And when prisoners are released, they may see better than most how fine is the line between inside and outside.

"We had all sorts of meetings that we don't dare hold outside," Nezam continued. "We got information about political activity anywhere. We received political publications I cannot get now. I'm sure the jailors knew, but they generally let us do whatever we wanted. Some of them even cooperated with us. During the year that Ghassan al-Jaba'i and I were together in Sadnaya, we formed what we called the Cultural Activities Committee. Once a week, we met at the end of the wing. Sometimes one of us would read a story he had just written. That was where I heard some of the stories that Ghassan later published in *Banana Fingers*. There were some political lectures. And once we adapted and put on *The Committee*."

"Do you mean the novel by the Egyptian Sonallah Ibrahim?"[1]

Nodding, he gave me a copy of the program that he had penned in his elegant hand. The notes described the theater and play as follows: "The place is constricted, conditions are so restricted they take theatricality out of theater. But . . . we still have great hope, and the fuel for this hope is you. We have left many gaps to be filled by the imagination and the culture of the spectator. Be gentle with our work, and please forgive us and help us." The tip of the hat to Shakespeare and the elevated, suggestive prose indicated an educated audience, fellow prisoners of conscience.

Nezam's program notes for prisoners' adaptation of Sonallah Ibrahim's *The Committee*.

"But how could you put on an entire play by someone like Sonallah Ibrahim, who is known to be a prison writer, without the jailors interfering?"

"They let us do whatever we wanted so long as we did not cause problems. One time we had a story reading session that went on for six hours. They even turned a blind eye when we started to brew our own beer and arak. Of course, if they wanted to get us for any reason, they used these forbidden activities as a pretext. I remember one time there was an alert while we were drinking our arak. In a panic we drank up our entire supply. Gulped it down. By the time they arrived we were so drunk we didn't much care what they did to us. Afterwards, though, we did care. I was in isolation for three weeks—that's hard. Every day, before every horrible meal, they beat me."

"How could you stand it, day after day?"

"Actually, you get used to it. With time, it gets to be the only way you know you're still alive."

"When I was talking with Ghassan, he told me that he never got to see the sunlight. But you tell me that you were free to move about."

"We could go outdoors twice a day for about ten minutes. They let us go out into the sahat al-tanaffus, where we marched in a line until our time was up. Some refused to go outside. Ghassan was one of them. But the time when we saw no natural light at all was in the Mezze Interrogation Center."

"Is that the famous Mezze jail?"

"Oh no! That prison up on the hill is the Sheraton! The Interrogation Center is underground. You know that area of the Mezze Ustrad that stretches between the College of Arts and the Customs for about two kilometers? Have you noticed that there are no buildings except for the university? Well, that road was our ceiling. During my whole year and a half—I think Ghassan was there for a year—I never once saw a beam of light from outside. The electric light was on around the clock. That was hell."

While he was talking, I shivered remembering how Ghassan had described the prison.

"Were you ever tempted to write?" I asked Nezam over hummus and tea.

"No. But many did. Some had written before, some wrote for the first time. Some of this writing is good and some of it is very bad."

He pulled off the shelves slim volumes that he handed to me. Leafing through a book, he would talk briefly about the author and curtly assess the writing.

"Sometimes you'll like someone very much but you have to admit that the book is just no good. Here's one, for example. Poor guy, he had to write it to deal with his feelings. Then there is someone like

Usama Aghi who's written some wonderful stories. Have you read him?"

I shook my head, and he gave me Usama Aghi's *Dismay* (1992). He insisted I take it despite the warm dedication to him and his brother, who had spent ten years inside.

"Have you seen the time? We've got to go!"

Two hours had passed like a flash and we were about to be late for our next appointment. We had to pick up some Ibn 'Arabi manuscript microfiches from the Asad Library. But before that we had to do something we had been planning for two months.

Just before leaving America, Bruce had been bitten by a copperhead, and a recent tetanus shot had saved him. In gratitude for his full recovery I had been encouraged to sacrifice a rooster or, if at all possible, a sheep. I kept delaying and ultimately decided to buy a chicken and give the meat to a poor family in Yarmuk.

"I'm afraid I'm very superstitious," I apologized to Nezam on our way to the chicken shop. "Do you find it weird?"

"No, not at all. We're very used to this kind of thing. We distribute food to the poor on all sorts of occasions, not just for illness but also to celebrate a happy event, like the return from the hajj or a marriage."

I bought the largest chicken in the shop, reminding myself that it was not the ritual but the gift of the meat that mattered. Winding our way through back alleys we finally came to the right area. We knocked on a door and asked for Umm Hasan. The young woman who answered the door seemed puzzled.

"Do you mean Abu Hasan?"

We exchanged amused glances. It was inconceivable to her that we should ask for Hasan's mother and not his father. In fact, she immediately knocked on her neighbor's door to tell her that these people had asked for Umm Hasan. Could she believe that?! As it turned out, there was no Abu Hasan. Dad had fled the family years before, leaving his wife and five children with nothing but his name. Umm Hasan's sister, also abandoned by her husband fifteen years earlier, had moved in with her, and they all lived off charity.

Nezam said, "That's what *zakat* means. This Islamic law, that demands of all believing Muslims that they give a percentage of their income to the poor, protects people like Umm Hasan whom the state neglects."

Next, we went to photocopy *The Committee* program that Nezam had penned while in prison. Hurrying along, we were talking again about the writers and filmmakers I had chosen for my project.

"Malas is very important. His films have been critical for us, especially *The Dream*. This documentary about the dreams of Palestinians living in the Lebanese camps of Sabra, Shatila, Burj al-Barajna, and 'Ain Hilwa has been an inspiration to us. And he is uncompromising. He's *ndif*, clean."

I had heard this "ndif" from several people when they were describing someone who had not sold out, who was ready to pay the price to say what had to be said. I wondered what he would say about Mamduh 'Adwan. Some accused him of being too close to the regime because of his connections with the Arab Writers Union.

"He's my teacher and a very good writer. Of course, he has more freedom than Malas, but he's ndif." (More free because he was Alawite?)

"What do you think of *The Ghoul*?"

"It was very courageous. The only problem's the language. It's a bit stilted. It's not so much that it's written in Qur'anic Arabic, but the characters spout Shakespearean speeches. Way too didactic! As you know, we're used to being entertained, and this play about tyranny and its consequences is too ideological to be really good theater. Mamduh's a good poet, but I'm not so sure about his plays. But I'm glad that you're working on Sa'adallah Wannus. I really admire his work. That's why I chose his *Historical Miniatures* to discuss with Doctor Bruce. Actually, you could compare this play with *The Ghoul*."

"That's what I'm planning to do. Don't you think that what 'Adwan and Wannus say about the past is relevant today?"

Maybe it was because it was my last day that I was being so open, or maybe because I felt an unprecedented trust. For whatever reason, I found myself talking more directly than ever before. After all, this was my last chance, since twenty-four hours later I would be back in North Carolina. Nezam did not seem at all shocked, but rather pleased that I was planning to write about dissidence and creativity in Hafiz Asad's Syria. His only problem with my research was that I was not taking into account the work of the younger generation. Why not?

"When I first came to Syria, I asked the writers I met who were the new voices to which I should listen. Since I had come to study the writings of women, the people I was meeting were Old Guard intellectuals like Colette al-Khuri and Ulfat Idilbi. They assured me that there was no new wave. I kept hearing that 1989 and the end of the Soviet system in the area had stifled literary and cultural initiatives. That's why I have chosen to limit the period of my study to the seven years between 1989 and 1996."

"Why 1996?"

"Because it's what I have personally experienced," I answered spontaneously, but it was a good question that I was to mull over during the following years. From the perspective of 2006, 1996 turned out to be the year that marked several ends. It was the end of the peace process for Syria. The election of the hard-liner Israeli prime minister, Benjamin Netanyahu, put an end to the hopes for normalization and the return of the Golan Heights. But 1996 was also the end of absolute control over the distribution of information. Satellite dishes were forbidden, yet they dotted the skyscape like a field of fungus. Many tapped into satellite programming with little fear of retribution and so BBC-World and CNN became the obvious choice over the state channels featuring Hafiz Asad shaking hands with the personality of the day. E-mail available across the globe was still not allowed into Syria.

"So my book will stretch between two ends: that of the Soviet hegemony and that of the American hope." I smiled to confirm the intended irony.

He looked at me "old-fashioned," as my mother used to say. What did I mean by "the American hope"?

I told Nezam about our first landlord, a retired general from the Syrian army, who'd said he was waiting for peace, for normalization, so that he might get the McDonald franchise. The living room, he would say, looking around the stiff space where we used to entertain him on his numerous and unannounced visits, would be the reception area. Then he would wander over to the bedroom and peer in curiously. Yes, the bedroom would be an office. From the bedroom the informal inspection would take him to the TV room, his pride and joy. There he had installed the best audiovisual equipment money could buy and, military general though he was, he had an illegal satellite dish. Every time he came to visit, he would make a beeline for the television, turn it on, and reprovingly ask why we were not watching Israel. I often wondered what would have happened if we had followed his advice and left the Israeli channel on. It was this man and his dreams that I meant when I talked about "the American hope."

Nezam was launching into a condemnation of the evils of American cultural imperialism and the contradictory hopes Syrians had invested in such enterprises as the McDonald's franchise, when two men came up to us.

"You've come at just the right moment," Nezam shouted. "I was talking with the Duktura about young writers and here you come. I'd like you to meet Nezam Nahawi and Wafiq Yusuf. This is Duktura Maryam. She's an American researching culture here, and she's been told that there are no young writers."

Yusuf invited us to his apartment. Although it was already one o'clock and I had stayed an hour longer than I should have, I decided to accept. We walked a couple of blocks to his building and then up several flights of breathless stairs. The place was immaculate and empty. He offered us something to drink and was disappointed that we would take only cold water.

"You have to write about what is going on here. We write and write and nothing leaves the country. I don't know why it is that we keep on, but we do. Maybe that's all we can do. Maybe that's how we survive. But for you it's different. You can write outside and tell the world what it's like here, and what we're doing. You risk nothing because as a foreigner you're protected."

Nothing? Not all outsiders risked nothing. I thought of Michel Seurat, the Frenchman born in the Tunisian port town of Bizerte whom Islamic Jihad had captured in Lebanon in 1985 and killed. In August 1947, when Michel was only fourteen, he saw some French parachutists massacre some Tunisians. He dedicated his life to expiating the crime. His wife, Marie Seurat, writes in her autobiography, *Corbeaux d'Alep*, that this crime revealed to Michel "his vocation of defender of just causes. It often annoyed me" (1988, 68). But not all were annoyed by such dedication; Don DeLillo was so intrigued he wrote *Mao II*. Marie remembers her husband saying, "Do whatever you can to make sure that after I'm released I do not have to leave this country. I've so much to do here. My guards and the group leader have promised to facilitate a move to the south. That's where I'll be able to finish my study of Shiite extremist groups" (91). He finished the study in the prison that finished him (see below).

Yusuf's exhortation to write reiterated what the French Institute critics had said months earlier: outsiders do have a role.

Before I left, Yusuf gave me a copy of the fall 1995 issue of the progressive Lebanese journal *Al-Tariq*. It was devoted to literary production inside Syria, and it featured the writings of fifteen young Syrians. Looking at the names I recognized only two, and they were there in the room with me. The *Al-Tariq* editor, Muhammad Kamil al-Khatib, called them the crest of a new wave. I was once again struck by the intensity of cultural activity that is so profoundly internalized in this somber country whose public culture revolves around the president and his two sons.

The next two hours were devoted to tying loose ends at the American Embassy, while Bruce said goodbye to Manhal Jamal, the Ibn 'Arabi "lover" who had become his spiritual guide. Twice a week for several weeks, we had gone to his room in the Shaikh Muhyi al-Din Ibn 'Arabi area where he lived with his wife and four children. He had chosen this area because it was just below the shrine, and he could visit al-Shaikh al-Akbar whenever he wanted. This "illiterate" man, as he called himself because he had not completed high school, had discoursed to us on the intricacies of the writings of the thirteenth-century al-Shaikh al-Akbar Ibn 'Arabi. He had died in Damascus, where his tomb remains a much frequented pilgrimage site. Manhal had situated Ibn 'Arabi's works within the Platonic and Aristotelian frame that was necessary to understand the philosophical underpinnings of his universalist mystical teachings. He had initiated us into what he called Akbarian devotional practices—Akbarian from al-Shaikh al-Akbar—like the invocation of some of God's Beautiful Names to be repeated daily 114 times for each chapter of the Qur'an. Finally I completed my chores and returned to pack. The phone rang.

"Hello."

"I've been trying to get hold of you all day. Tell me, how is the packing? Are you done?"

"No, I've just gotten out of the shower. What's up, Muhammad? You've got something on your mind." I could sense excitement in Malas's voice.

"I've been phoning since noon. The Michel Seurat film has turned up!"

"Okay, I'm coming!"

Malas and 'Umar Amiralay had been working on the film for several years. The film was being produced in Paris and it had looked as though I was going to miss it. But then came this stroke of luck.

My hair still wet, I flung on some clothes to face the street and micro again. It was 105 degrees, bone dry and dusty. For the next-to-last time, my stomach churning, I rushed over the Mezze Interrogation Center, under the bridge decorated with huge posters of the president and large red hearts donated by the Dentists Union, and then up to Rawda Square and on to the palace and past the guards. I sat down in front of the tiny television and Malas started the film. While the color stripes lingered on the screen, I asked him if he liked it. He smiled a rare, almost happy, smile but said nothing. The title appeared: *Par un jour de violence ordinaire: Mon ami, Michel Seurat.*

The first scene is of an empty prison bed with Amirallay's voice-over asking Michel, "How do I make a film of you without opening up all our old wounds?" Malas and Amiralay made the film to answer some of the questions that Michel's father, who died of shock when he heard of his son's death, had not had the time to ask. Still speaking to Michel, Amiralay explains that the elder Seurat had died "without knowing what you were doing in your distant Middle East and why you were killed." At that point, the screen is cut with an arch, a white space framed in black, like a cave entrance. Slowly and ominously, silhouettes with Kalashnikovs rise up out of the ground to fill the light-drenched opening. These are the men from Islamic Jihad who captured Michel and Jean-Paul Kauffmann, a French journalist from the weekly *l'Événement de jeudi*, upon their landing in Beirut. The film is told from his perspective.

They hid Michel for seven months in a basement cell somewhere in Beirut while his wife Marie rushed from one Shiite military leader to another to plead her husband's case. The film alternates interviews with some of Michel's friends, his wife Marie, Amiralay and Kauffmann, who survived the ordeal to join in the film project. Kaufmann dully details the deadly dailiness of captivity, the memoirs of ordinary violence. The Jihad militiamen were "morbid, suspicious, completely identified with the organization; they have lost touch with reality. They're inflexible and stupid." Again and again, he went back to that word "stupid." This is not anger, but frustration. On the 30 August 1985, Islamic Jihad released their hostage for a single night that he spends with Marie: "gulping for air, his chest dilates as though to allow his heart to beat more strongly. . . . Then he bursts into tears. I had never seen him cry" (Seurat 1988, 54, 87–88).

In the film Marie narrates this return in the monotone that marks all the interviews: "He embraced me tightly, too tightly. I felt his heart beat against my ribs like the whips at Ashura." Toward the end of the film, we see and hear a scene from Ashura: men beating themselves and moaning in ritual commemoration of the seventh-century murder in Karbala of Husain, the grandson of the Prophet Muhammad. This scene, projected after the narrative has progressed beyond Michel's death, recalls the wildness of his heartbeat when he embraces Marie for the last time.[2]

"This was not Michel," she says in the film, leaning against the doorframe, exhausted by the memory. Two days later, Michel came down with hepatitis, and the guards did nothing, beyond clucking an impatient "Basita!," which means something like "Take it easy!"

"It was this *basita* that killed him," Kauffmann says flatly and the screen fills with the grisly sight of Michel's death's-head. Islamic Jihad released a photograph of his cadaver to confirm his death. Images cover other images, Qur'ans, photographs of Michel's death mask, and the sea surging in to drown out all symbols of the prison. The last to go are the bars. The sea washes over the prison bed and bars strewn over the Beirut beach. Death releases Michel.

At 9:30, back in our apartment, Malas and his wife turned up to say goodbye, and within minutes Mamduh ʿAdwan and his wife, Ilham. We sat out in the garden and talked about each other's projects and when we would meet again.

The phone rang twice. The first was a colleague from Damascus University who had spent nine months in Durham, North Carolina. She had called me Maryuma and my father Daddy. She had shown me every word she wrote. She had told me how beautiful her country was and how I would love it. But when I turned up she disappeared. My initial shock that she would not, could not(?) see me while I was in her city gave way to indifference. I had read her weekly columns to keep up with her official preoccupations: pollution, expensive schoolbooks, and the Zionist enemy. Others excused her distance by saying that she had been swept up into government service upon her return from the United States, a way of sanitizing the American interlude. So when I arrived in Damascus, she had been too nervous to see much of me. She told me how sorry she was that she had not been able to see me, had not been able to take better care of me. I was happy she called.

The second call was from Manhal Jamal. It was almost midnight and he had not wanted me to go without saying goodbye. "Is there anything you want to say to me?" he asked. With our friends outside in the garden and the night advancing toward our predawn departure, I didn't know quite how to respond. Suddenly, I was sad to leave these wonderful people who live their austere lives so fully, so gracefully.

We used to welcome the sleep of the tyrant
as though hoping that the Slaughterer
might die in his sleep
But nowadays
the tyrant even if he's dead he sleeps
Tyranny follows its course
even after the tyrants go
We must not delude ourselves
that the death of the tyrant
guarantees the people's happiness
But the tyrant
even when he inspires fear he himself fears
a fear in a tyrant
is like a wandering ghost
It appears only in dreams . . .
Who will abort him out of the womb of the future?
The greatest danger
from this tyrant
is that he will recur
—MAMDUH 'ADWAN, *The Ghoul*

postscript

When Bashar Asad took over power upon his father's death in 2000 many hoped that things would change. And in the early, heady days of the son's rule it looked as though these hopes might be realized. This early period was called the "Damascus Spring." On 28 May 2000, the writer Michel Kilo, who had been jailed between 1980 and 1983, invited intellectuals to the home of the film director Nabil Malih to discuss how to "revive the cultural and democratic movement in Syria. . . . The group established itself formally as a Constituent Board for . . . the Committees for the Revival of Civil Society in Syria" (George 2003, 33). Not only were such intellectual forums allowed, but the "infamous Mezzeh political prison was closed, and hundreds of long-imprisoned dissidents released. An opposition press sprouted, and eminent political cartoonist 'Ali Farzat won the Dutch Prince Claus Award for achievement in culture and development" (Salamandra 2004, 158).

During the Damascus Spring, periods of unprecedented liberalization seemed to make room for dissident voices, the release of political prisoners from the Muslim Brotherhood and the Communist Action Party, the proliferation of independent media outlets, and even a reconstructed banking system. On 27 September 2000 the London-based daily *al-Hayat* published "The Statement of 99." The ninety-nine in question were Syrian intellectuals, artists, and professionals who included Mamduh 'Adwan, Adonis, Sadiq al-'Azm, 'Abd al-Rahman Munif, Muhammad Malas, 'Umar Amiralay, Usama Muhammad, 'Abd al-Latif 'Abd al-Hamid, Shawqi Baghdadi, and Michel Kilo. They were demanding an end to the State of Emergency that had been in place since 1963, the pardon of political prisoners and exiles, and the establishment of a " 'state of law' that would recognize 'political and intellectual pluralism' " (George 2003, 39).

But this openness did not last long. In early 2001 the state cracked down on opposition voices and ushered in what came to known as the "Damascus Winter." Leading civil society advocates were arrested and "human rights organizations estimate that thousands [of political prisoners] remain in Syrian jails, and there have been reports of systematic torture. . . . Bashar Asad kept intact a state-security arm that can strike without notice" (Glain 2005, 67–68). President Bashar came down hard on intellectuals who had been overreaching in their demands. In a 9 February 2001 interview published by *al-Sharq al-Awsat*, he said that Syria's intellectuals were "a small group which portrays itself as an elite. [It was] entirely unnatural for them to be truly representative of the majority. [It was] only natural for [me] not to be swayed by what is said by a few people here and there. It is obvious that there are great differences between the priorities of most of our people and what this group is advocating" (George 2003, 49). Clearly things had moved too fast for the young president. But the intellectuals continued to meet and to demand an end to the State of Emergency, among other political reforms. The government responded with arrests of civil society movement leaders.

In an interview with Alan George in July 2002 Patrick Seale said, "As a lifelong friend and student of Syria, I'm extremely sorry that hopes for President Bashar have not been realized. It's a tragedy that Syria has reverted to its former immobility on the domestic front" (George 2003, xiii). And the cartoonist 'Ali Farzat told a foreign reporter, "'We are like someone in the bathroom who finds the water is hot one minute and cold the next.' . . . Change is there, but it has been overshadowed by what remains the same" (Salamandra 2004, 158–159). Farzat's description of hot and cold water recalls Samu'il's description of life in Hafiz Asad's Syria.

The works and strategies of Sa'adallah Wannus, Muhammad Malas, Mamduh 'Adwan, Ghassan al-Jaba'i, Faraj Bairaqdar, Ibrahim Samu'il, Muhammad Maghut, and Nadia Khust remain relevant today, providing models of creative opposition to autocratic rule. They teach us in the United States in 2006 that we have to take seriously those who call for freedom and democracy, however preposterous their rhetoric, however blatant their deceptive sloganeering. Plays, films, and writings about jails, both real and virtual, produced during the last years of Hafiz Asad's reign are increasingly relevant to Americans dealing with the mystifications of George W. Bush, who peppered his January 2005 inaugural address to his second term in office with "freedoms" and "democracies." I wondered at the time why this sounded so familiar and then I remembered Maghut's buffoon. The earnest man had gone out shopping for freedom, and the freedom vendor told him that freedom of expression was sold out, but that there was plenty of "freedom of import and export" still for sale (Maghut 2001, 128). Yes, Bush believes in free trade (Neier 2004) and, more ominously than Maghut's intellectual, he believes in his God-given freedom to take preemptive action where he sees fit.[1] Žižek notes that when Bush says "Freedom is not America's gift to other nations, it is God's gift to humanity," he is speaking "in the best totalitarian fashion [because] those who oppose the leader do not only oppose him, they also oppose the deepest and noblest aspirations of the people . . . rejecting God's noblest gift to humanity" (2004, 25–26).

Syrian dissidents mocked such mystifications. In March 1992 a Syrian martial court sentenced the journalist and founding member of the Committee for the Defense of Democratic Freedom Nizar Nayyuf to ten years hard labor for "disseminating false information." In fact, he had helped to "found the Committees for the Defense of Democratic Freedoms and Human Rights (CDF) and to edit their monthly newsletter" (George 2003, 122). He had also written an article critical of the 1991 elections that could apply to George W. Bush's project for Iraq and the Middle East (see Feldman 2004, 92–129). Entitled "Democracy Has Come . . . and the Democrats Are Nowhere to Be Seen," the article demanded the release of all prisoners of conscience and accused the government of "legalized fraud and engaging in constructing conditions that allow only those in favor of their regime to vote. . . . An abnormal state of affairs is smothering the country, rendering a true electoral campaign impossible" (quoted in Dowd 1993, 61). After his release in 2001 Nayyuf remained under surveillance and his family was threatened. American PEN, UNESCO, and Human Rights Watch honored him for his activism and his poetry.

The conditions for cultural production during the last years of Hafiz Asad's rule provide an unexpected prism through which to read public discourse in the United States since the Gulf War, and more than ever since the U.S. occupation of Iraq in 2003. National security was the pretext the Syrian state used to target its civilians, just as it is today for the U.S. government to harass people from the Middle East, people of Middle Eastern heritage, and scholars of the Middle East who exercise their constitutional right to freedom of thought and expression and who refuse to buy into the Bush Doctrine.[2]

What is at stake in George W. Bush's United States, as it was in Asad's Syria, is control of intellectuals through sloganeering. In both cases, the nation in extreme distress is invoked in order to align education and culture with the national project. In her account of the roles of institutions and individuals in shaping the Nazi conscience, Claudia Koonz has revealed how dangerous was the aligning of education with nationalist aspirations (2003, 55).

How can Middle East specialists continue to function in such an environment? We are caught in a double bind that tries to silence us. If we criticize Arab regimes we may seem to condone military interference in the affairs of so-called rogue states. If we don't, we are called apologists and anti-American and, therefore, a threat to national security. We are dangerous and therefore worthy targets for neocon harassment (Horowitz 2006). How are we to make our research and writing an instrument of justice and peace? How can we critique the tyranny of rulers like Hafiz Asad without falling into the arms of the jingoistic patriots? How can we criticize our government and its Middle East policies without being stigmatized as treasonous? While I do not have adequate answers, these questions have haunted the writing of this book.

Those who dare to criticize the Syrian state and to sign their names to their writings risk being silenced if they cannot be heard outside the environment that suppresses or co-opts them. The world sees people like the Syrians and Iraqis as crushed by their governments, at best unable to resist, at worst actively complicit and, therefore, part of the problem. Yet the resistance is everywhere and as strong as the line between dissidence and martyrdom allows it to be. Salman Rushdie urges international intellectuals to magnify the voices of Arab, Afghan, Latin American, and Russian dissidents in George W. Bush's United States "so that they can be heard loud and clear just as the Soviet dissidents once were. . . . It has perhaps never been more important for the world's voices to be heard in America, never more important for the world's ideas and dreams to be known and thought about and discussed, never more important for a global dialogue to be fostered" (2005, 31). To magnify their voices is to highlight commonalities across national, cultural, and linguistic borders that allow us to draw lessons from the strangest of places.

Living in truth entails solidarity with all who demand justice. To challenge the obscenity of power, dissidents under threat should know that the international intelligentsia is listening and participating in a collective project of resistance by taking these texts out of their controlled environment and making them part of an international agenda. Faraj Bairaqdar acknowledges that it was the international campaign by Amnesty International, Journalists without Borders, and International PEN that led to his release. The attention of outsiders can break the closed circuit between the actor and the one acted upon, between an authoritarian regime and its people, whether in 1990s Syria or in the twenty-first-century United States.

It is not easy to keep resisting when, like a roller coaster, the cycle of violence soars and dips. In December 2002 Riyadh al-Turk, whom some call Syria's Nelson Mandela, saluted his supporters who demonstrated outside the State Security Court where he was being held: "It's a proof that the state of hiding and silence has begun to fall apart, which is an important sign for the future of the democratic movement in Syria" (quoted in Atassi 2004, 14). But this optimism did not last long: in June 2004 Samir Kassir, the editor in chief of the Lebanese *Al-Nahar* and outspoken critic of Syria, was killed; the next year two more anti-Syrian Lebanese, Prime Minister Hariri and the *Al-Nahar* editor Jibran Tueni, were assassinated. And the situation worsened.

Syrian dissidents are not giving up. On his deathbed the journalist Reda Haddad wrote that after he left prison, though it had not left him, his "spirit is still yearning towards freedom, dignity and justice" (quoted in Atassi 2004, 8). This irrepressible urge to live and to witness and to live in truth can be heard in Bairaqdar's words: "The freedom within us is larger than the prisons that we're in" (12).

I close this book with a poem composed by a friend with whom I have spent many hours talking about this book:

> She asked me about dictators in my land
> My tongue, for a while, being long constrained
> Was helpless, captured in its cage.
> When you do not use it, you lose it, they say
> And I have lost my tongue out of disuse.
>
> But the sky was different where we sat
> On students' benches
> The trees were shimmering with a thousand lights
> The leaves were turning in glorious hues
> The young were passing us by
> Chattering at ease on recent news

I recalled imprisoned tongues, fettered cheeks, zipped mouths
The sad gaze in bottomless eyes
Words assassinated before they were born
Thoughts slain before they materialized
The dead alive in my ancient city of
Thousands of years

The air got lighter all of a sudden
The breeze was lulling me into amnesia
For a moment, I did not recall
The prison and the prisoner
And told it all
To the foreign lady on the bench

Anon

notes

Introduction

1 H. Bruce Franklin has written similarly of African American prison literature, lauding its contribution to U.S. culture: "The songs of slavery metamorphosed into the songs of prison, and scores of African-American convict artists then transmuted those collective prison songs into individual works that shaped the blues tradition at the heart of much 20th century American music" (1998, 6).

2 Ibn Taymiyya (1263–1328) was a religious scholar of the Hanbali School of jurisprudence who lived between Syria and Egypt. He was very critical of any deviation from what he considered to be orthodox Sunni Islam, including Shiism and some aspects of Sufism. He remains an authority today for some Islamic fundamentalists.

3 In 1970 Khalil Brayez, a former captain and intelligence officer in

the army, was imprisoned for writing two novels (*The Fall of the Golan* and *From the Golan Files*) critical of the Syrian army's performance during the 1967 war. He was released twenty-eight years later in May 1998 (www .amnesty.org/ailib/aireport/ar99/mde24.htm, accessed February 2005).

4 They made Ayyub Badri change the female Muslim lead in his 1928 *Al-muttaham al-bari'* (The innocent accused) because they did not want films to present Muslim women in a positive light. In 1932, they stopped the production of 'Atta Makka's *Taht sama' Dimashq* (Under the Damascus sky), with the pretext that Makka had not paid "fees for pre-recorded music that accompanied the film" (Shafik 1998, 15).

5 See Article 3(e) of Legislative Decree No. 6 of 7 January 1965, quoted in HRW/ME 1995, 16.

6 The mosaic of Hafiz Asad and his mother might seem to some problematic in a religion that frowns upon the representation of humans, especially in a mosque.

7 It is here that the head of the Prophet's grandson Husain is buried.

8 Thanks to Oleg Grabar for pointing out this detail to me during his tour of inspection of the restoration for UNESCO (conversation in December 1995).

9 Thanks to Tolly Boatwright for drawing my attention to the connection with Roman inscriptions.

10 For accounts of the Hama affair, see Kienle (1994), Van Dam (1996). Several anonymous books appeared in the 1980s detailing the massacre and including names and numbers of dead and photographs documenting the destruction: *Majzarat Hama: al-qissa al-haqiqiya bi al-asma' wa al-waqai'wa al-arqam wa al-suwar li akbar majzara fi al-'asr al-hadith* (The Hama massacre: The true story with names, events, statistics and images of the worst massacre in modern times) (Cairo: Dar al-I'tisam, 1984/1987).

11 Some of these cases attracted international attention: Human Rights Watch and Amnesty International have made special appeals on behalf of some detainees: in 1980, Muhammad Khoja and Wadi Ismandar (see *Index*, July 1987); in 1981, Wa'il al-Sawah; in 1982, Jamil Hatmal (*Index on Censorship*, February 1984, June 1987); in 1987, Mustafa Hussein and the poet Faraj Ahmad Bairaqdar; in 1992, the Palestinian Salama George Kila and the Kurd Ahmed Hasso. In 1991, the poet Munir al-Ahmad was arrested and died in custody (*Index on Censorship*, September 1992).

12 It is estimated that in 1996 there were about 2,700 political prisoners in Syrian jails (Wedeen 1999, 27). Barbara Harlow writes that the United States also claims that there are no political prisoners in its numerous jails (1992, 201).

13 Sham means Damascus and more generally Syria.

14 www.nobelprize.org/nobel_prizes/literature/laureates/1949/ (accessed 14 September 2006).

Chapter One. "Culture Is Humanity's Highest Need"

1 Albert Camus, *The Rebel*, translated by Anthony Bower (New York: Penguin, 1953), 28.

2 Describing the Iraqi Baath constitution, Ziauddin Sardar writes that, like its Syrian counterpart, it "declares 'freedom of speech, freedom of assembly, freedom of belief, and freedom of art are sacred things which no authority can diminish.' . . . The freedom of speech, publication and assembly belongs to the state—the citizens are at its mercy!" (2004, 109).

3 In his October 1995 report, Qayyim listed the achievements of the Corrective Movement: 103 cultural centers, 141 libraries, 48 academies of popular culture. Whereas the government in 1963 was publishing thirteen books a year, by 1995 the number had increased to 125 "in all fields and all subjects." The ministry published six cultural journals; theatrical initiatives were offered in Damascus and other cities; literacy rates had increased from 37 percent in 1960 to 79 percent in 1993; the number of archaeological sites and museums had increased; the film industry and its status had also increased; and there were many cultural festivals, including book and film festivals in Damascus and the popular arts festival in Busra.

4 In his lexical exploration of culture, Eagleton found that its Latin root *colere* "can mean anything from cultivating and inhabiting to *worshipping* and protecting . . . *colere* also ends up via the Latin *cultus* as the religious term 'cult.' . . . If religion offers cult, sensuous symbolism, social unity, collective identity, a combination of practical morality and spiritual idealism, and a link between the intellectuals and the populace, so does culture" (2000, 2, 40–41; my emphasis). Latin ties these two words together so that culture is not wildly amorphous but specific; it is connected with cult.

5 During the 1970s and 1980s Maghut collaborated with the comedian Durayd Lahham to produce political satires like *Kasak ya watan* (Cheers, homeland, 1979) and films like *Al-taqrir* (The report, 1986). For a discussion of these films, see Wedeen (1999, 93–99).

Chapter Two. Our Literature Does Not Leave the Country

1 All who wrote about this war were assumed to be patriots, even when they criticized the war, for example, Muhammad Walid al-Hafiz's *Al-khandaq* (The trench, 1985), which he dedicated to all the fighters who would not make it into the history books. Nadia Khust sees the novel as a symbolic call for confrontation with Israel (*Tishrin*, 27 February 1986). 'Ali al-Maz'al praised Hafiz's critical collection, *Al-midfa 'al-khamis* (The fifth cannon, 1989), for its patriotism (*Al-Baath*, 22 December 1991). For an overview of this war literature, see 'Id (1993, 251–267).

Chapter Three. No Such Thing as Women's Literature

1 For a discussion of these works, see Salamandra (2004, 128–130).

2 The playwright and critic Riyad 'Ismat later gave me a copy of one of his weekly columns in the *Al-Baath* daily newspaper entitled "The Feminine Imagination." He had written it several weeks prior to the nadwa. In it he argues that the very term "women's literature" implies a value judgment, one that is unfavorable to women. Whereas there can be many men occupying their own spaces on the literary stage, there is room for only one woman. To be there she must be deemed the best, to the exclusion of the others. Walid Midfa'i's (1996) analysis of Mallahat al-Khani's three volumes of short stories is an example of this zero-sum attitude. He writes that this woman's work is absolutely richer and deeper than that of other women, who are therefore jealous of her.

Chapter Four. Commissioned Criticism

1 Human Rights Watch described the six parties, along with the official Baath Party, that acted out the pretense of democracy, as serving to project the "image of political pluralism" (HRW/ME 1995, 10).

2 For example, 'Abd al-Latif 'Abd al-Hamid's film *Layali ibn Awa* (Hyena nights) and Ghassan al-Jaba'i's story of a man pinned under his upturned car and surrounded by hyenas awaiting his death (1994, 35–38).

3 "The Ba'thist process of state formation was guided in its early years by a more determined effort to repress the private sector, ensure the domination of capital by the state, and break the autonomy of traditional elites and the new bourgeoisie" (Heydemann 1999, 132).

Chapter Five. Dissident Performances

1 Several writers have chosen to title plays and stories "The Ghoul." See Ibrahim Samu'il's short story about an abusive father in this 1990 collection *Light Coughs*, and Ghassan al-Jaba'i's story about a vicious jailor that the Ministry of Culture would not allow to be published in his 1994 collection *Banana Fingers* (see chapter 7).

2 "It is not impossible that he thought him [Tamerlane] the man of the century who had enough 'asabiya to reunite the Muslim world and to give hisotry a new direction." Ibn Khaldun counsels city dwellers against jihad because their life of luxury does not "inspire any willingness to die. [They] have little endurance. The turmoil of battle frightens them, and their lines crumble" (Ibn Khaldun 1969, 227). Above all, this life of luxury cannot produce effective leaders. See also Fischel (1952).

3 In the *Muqaddimah* we read, "Scholars are, of all people, those least familiar with the ways of politics. The reason for this is that scholars are used to mental speculation and to a searching study of ideas which they abstract from the *sensibilia* and conceive in their minds as general universals, so that they be applicable to some matter in general but not to any particular matter, individual, race, nation, or group of people" (Ibn Khaldun 1969, 427).

4 'Abd al-Rahman Munif gives a historical background to Ibn Khaldun's shocking act of betrayal. Sultan Abu 'Inan had imprisoned Ibn Khaldun with others for conspiracy against him. He had refused clemency until Ibn Khaldun wrote him a panegyric two hundred lines long (Munif 1996, 120). His hypocritical writing gave him his freedom.

5 "After having written for Tamerlane a description of the Maghreb and having witnessed the horrors of the burning and pillaging of Damascus, he returned to Cairo . . . and, despite his compromising attitude toward the Mongol leader, he was well received in court."

Chapter Six. Filming Dreams

1 In the mid-1990s there were only twenty theaters in Damascus and ninety in the whole of Syria (Kennedy-Day 2001, 390). The films screened in the al-Kindi Theater included some of the greats of Syrian film history: Usama Muhammad's *Nujum al-nahar* (Stars of the day, 1988), 'Abd al-Hamid's *Layali Ibn Awa* (Jackal nights, 1989), Malas's *Ahlam al-madina* (City dreams, 1984), and Durayd Laham's *Al-taqrir* (The report, 1986).

2 See Walid Hammami in *Jeune Afrique*, 22 October 1992; Badr (1987,

44). vGIK was the academy that trained several other Syrian filmmakers, including 'Abd al-Latif 'Abd al-Hamid, Usama Muhammad, Raymond Butrus, and Samir Zikra.

3 See Muhammad Ibn Rajab, "Dreams of the City: A New Film from Syria Whose Strength Is in Its Simplicity," *al-Sabah*, 18 October 1984. Although the auteur "supposedly died years ago . . . within the startlingly vibrant and utterly distinctive realm of Syrian cinema . . . authorship remains not only conceivable but necessary" (Stuart Klawans, "Wind from the Mideast," *The Nation*, 5 June, 2006).

4 In an article written for the Syrian Film Festival held in New York in May 2006, Richard Pena, the program director of the Film Society of Lincoln Center, writes of *City Dreams*: "Exquisitely made and directed, the film offered one of the most skillful weavings of personal story and historical consciousness that I had ever seen." He calls *The Night* "simply a masterpiece. . . . Its innovative blending of personal and historical narratives was even more provocative, and his style was further enhanced by various surrealist touches. Clearly, something was going on in the Syrian cinema" (www.filmlinc.com/wrt/onsale/syriano6/richard_pena.html, accessed 20 September 2006).

5 When, in 1992, *Night* won the Tanit d'Or in Carthage, "the Syrian film world basked in the reflected glory of this triumph, yet the film was never screened in Syria's own film festivals" (Porteous 1995, 209; HRW 1991, 129–130). Malas told Hala Abdallah in 1984 that "foreign film festivals are more interested in Arab films than are the Arabs" (*al-Mawqif al-'Arabi* 10 July 1984).

6 Before *City Dreams* Malas made several shorts, including *Dream of a Small City* (1972), *Kuneitra* (1974), and *Memory*" (1975).

7 For cinematographer Robert Bresson, what matters in films "is not what they show me but what they hide from me and, above all, *what they do not suspect is in them*. . . . Let it be the feelings that bring about the events. Not the other way. . . . Hide the ideas, but so that people find them. The most important will be the most hidden" (1986, 4–5, 28, 34).

8 This is also the story of *al-Tirhal* (Exodus, 1997) by the Syrian Orthodox Raymond Butros. The hero is the largely absent husband, a sculptor, who has gone to Palestine to fight. Upon his return, government forces capture him for sheltering a neighbor whom they consider to be a political activist. Again, Syrian authorities punish an Arab nationalist.

9 In her novel *Zaina* Wisal Samir writes about the forbiddenness of dreaming: "You know perfectly well that poor people like us are not allowed to dream. . . . My only crime was that I was walking while dream-

ing" (1992, 67, 73) And when a truck driver runs over a boy, he declares, "I didn't kill a child. . . . The criminal is the dream so you should try the dream. . . . The disaster befell me after I had dreamt that Faysal had become a successful doctor, Faruq a successful engineer, Fuad a businessman and Fadia a journalist. It was then that I drowned in the dream" (78–79).

10 Sabah al-Jazairi, lead actress in *Night*, called Malas' filmmaking "writing poetry with a camera." For Stephen Holden, a film critic for the *New York Times*, *Night* was "almost impenetrable" (4 October 1993).

11 Liana Badr praised Malas for going beyond the physical ugliness of the camps to draw out their beauty and pathos. The cemetery "is paradise on earth toward which the mothers extend their arms with tender longing for their children" (Badr 1987, 43). Despair is so total in those places that martyrdom is the only hope.

12 In 1928 Ayyub Badri produced *Al-muttaham al-bari'* (The innocent accused), the first Syrian film (Shafik 1998, 15). Rashid Jalal and Ismail Anzur had produced and directed silent movies in the early 1930s, but Shahbandar was the first to make a film with sound.

13 "The 'paradox' of Syrian cinema is that so many of these state-financed pictures really are provocations—beautiful, strange, uncanny provocations" (Klawans, "Wind from the Mideast," *The Nation*, 5 June 2006).

Chapter Seven. Lighten Your Step

1 Until the eighteenth century the British and French used model surveillance mechanisms and institutions, including the underground prison, or oubliette, as it was called in Le Chatelet prison (Slyomovics 2005, 95).

2 It is curious that a Christian would use the word *barzakh*, which is most commonly associated with the Qur'anic verse 23: 100 referring to the barrier between life and death that is both life and death and neither.

3 This is true elsewhere. Moroccan prisoners writing before 1999 about their time in the infamous prison of Tazmamart could not indicate where they had written (Slyomovics 2005).

4 Ervand Abrahamian describes similar conditions in the notorious Evin prison in Iran, where for months and sometimes years there would be so little room that "inmates took turns sleeping on the floor—each person rationed to three hours of sleep every twenty-four hours" (1999, 140). Rooms built for twelve might hold up to ninety (169).

5 Aesop's Arab equivalent is 'Abdallah Ibn al-Muqaffa' (d. 756). The translator from Persian to Arabic of a collection of animal fables entitled *Kalila* and *Dimna*, he is credited with introducing into the Islamic literary and philosophical traditions "the idea of voicing criticism of revealed religion and of human society and morality through the mouths of animals" (Bosworth 1983, 487).

6 Mustafa Tlas, former minister of defense, affirmed that every week during the 1980s there might be as many as 150 hangings in Damascus alone (Koelbl 2005, 113).

7 By May 2006 conditions in Guantánamo prison had so deteriorated that a United Nations panel that monitors compliance with the Convention Against Torture called for its closure (Tim Golden, "U.S. Should Close Prison in Cuba, U.N. Panel Says," *New York Times*, 20 May 2006).

Chapter Eight. Leaving Damascus

1 Ibrahim is best known for the 1966 collection of short stories about prison entitled *The Smell of It*. The title story, set in the authoritarian world of Nasser's Egypt, tells of the return of a prisoner to his home and the terrible disappointments that await him.

2 Marie attends Ashura two weeks later in Bir Abed. Inside a cramped space are women and children; outside "men in black tunics with gold cardboard swords collapse on the asphalt" (Seurat 1988, 114).

Postscript

1 "The Bush administration understands the words 'tyranny' and 'freedom' in much the same way as it understands international law. They mean whatever the White House wants them to mean" (G. Younge, "A Fantasy of Freedom," *Guardian Weekly*, 28 January –2 February 2005, 15).

2 The Bush Doctrine gives the president "unilateral powers to: launch a major, pre-emptive invasion without congressional approval; to order the indefinite detention of any and all people he alleges to be 'enemy combatants' (including Americans seized on American soil) without due process or access to lawyers or courts; authorize indiscriminate torture to make such detainees talk, in defiance of international treaty obligations and a 1994 law making torture a crime" (Taylor 2006, 26). As David Palumbo-Liu writes, "The abandonment of deterrence in favor of preemption" turns uncertainty into a reason for action in order to maintain hegemony; it "must always seek out threat in order to reanimate itself. It must imag-

ine always a potential state of (its own) weakness as a pretext to reassert its strength." He continues, citing Richard Falk, "'It is a doctrine without limits, without accountability to the UN or international law, without any dependence on a collective judgment of responsible governments and, what is worse, without any convincing demonstration of practical necessity'" (2006, 151–152).

bibliography

'Abbas, Hassan, and Ahmad Maala. 2005. *Dalil al-muwatana* (Citizenship guide). Damascus: Ministry of Information Censorship Bureau.

Abrahamian, Ervand. 1999. *Tortured Confessions: Prisons and Public Recantations in Modern Iran.* Berkeley: University of California Press.

Adnan, Taha. 2004. "Al-sha'ir al-suri Faraj Bairaqdar: 'Adad al-siyat allati talaqqaituha yu'adil 'adad al-kalimat allati katabtuha" (The Syrian poet Faraj Bairaqdar: The number of whiplashes I received is equal to the number of words I wrote). *Al-Quds al-Arabi.*

Adonis [pseud. of 'Ali Ahmad Sa'id]. 1977. *Al-thabit wa al-mutahawwil* (The permanent and the changing). Beirut: Dar al-'Awda.

'Adwan, Mamduh. 1996. *Al-Ghul: Jamal Pasha al-saffah* (The Ghoul: Jamal Pasha the butcher). Damascus: Arab Writers Union Publications.

Aghi, Usama. 1992. *Dhuhul* (Dismay). Damascus: Dar al-Ilm.

'Alim, Mahmud Amin al-. 1996. "Qira'at li-Munamnamat tarikhiya wa surat Ibn Khaldun" (Readings of *Historical Miniatures* and the image of Ibn Khaldun). *Al-Tariq* 1.1 (January–February): 105–116.

Amnesty International. 1995. "Syria: Repressions and Impunity. The Forgotten Victims." *AI Index*, April. http://web.amnesty.org/library/index/.

Arab Writers Union. 1978. *Hafiz al-Asad wa qadaya al-kitaba wa al-kuttab* (Hafiz Asad and issues concerning writing and writers). Damascus: Arab Writers Union Publications.

Arendt, Hannah. 1979 [1948]. *The Origins of Totalitarianism.* New York: Harcourt Brace.

Atassi, Mohammad Ali. 2004. "The Other Prison." *Al-Nahar Cultural Supplement*, 11 July. Translated by Kamal Dib in *Al-Jadid* 10.49.

————. 2001. "Words behind Bars: Syrian Poet Faraj Bairaqdar Speaks after Fourteen Years of Detention." Interview in *Al-Nahar Cultural Supplement*, 22 January. Translated anonymously in *Al-Jadid* 10.49 (2004).

Badr, Liana. 1987. "Baina al-jamaliya wa al-trajidiya: Manam wa hulm ʿan Filastin" (Between aesthetics and tragedy: *Dream* and dreaming about Palestine). *Al-Hurriya* 5.3.

Badran, Margot, and miriam cooke, eds. 2004. *Opening the Gates: Arab Feminist Writings.* Bloomington: Indiana University Press.

Banha, Colette. 1995. *Al-iʾtiraf al-awwal* (The first confession). Damascus: Dar al-Talia al-Jadida.

Barqawi, Ahmad. 1999. "Naqd al-hadatha al-ʿarabiya: Idiyulujiya al-hadatha al-ʿarabiya al-rahina wa naqduha" (Critique of Arab modernism: Critique of the ideology of contemporary Arab modernism). *Al-Adab*, January.

Benaissa, Zinelabidine. 1995. "La roue, l'eau et le vent." In *Cinecrits: Spécial "La Nuit" de Mohamed Malas*, edited by Tahar Chikhaoui. Tunis: Editions Sahar.

Benjamin, Walter. 1968. *Illuminations: Essays and Reflections.* New York: Schocken.

Bodel, John, ed. 2001. *Epigraphic Evidence: Ancient History from Inscriptions.* New York: Routledge.

Bosworth, C. E. 1983. "The Persian Impact on Arabic Literature." In *Arabic Literature to the End of the Umayyad Period*, edited by A. F. L. Beeston, T. M. Johnstone, R. B. Serjeant, and G. R. Smith. Cambridge: Cambridge University Press.

Bresson, Robert. 1986 [1975]. *Notes on the Cinematographer.* Translated by Jonathan Griffin. London: Quartet.

Chakravarty, Sumita S. 2003. "The Erotics of History: Gender and Transgression in the New Asian Cinemas." In *Rethinking Third Cinema*, edited

by Anthony R. Guneratne and Wimal Dissanayake. New York: Routledge.

Chikhaoui, Tahar. 1995. "Les incertitudes de la nuit." In *Cinecrits: Spécial
"La Nuit" de Mohamed Malas*, edited by Tahar Chikhaoui. Tunis: Editions Sahar.

cooke, miriam, and Angela Woollacott, eds. 1993. *Gendering War Talk*.
Princeton, N.J.: Princeton University Press.

Dandashli, Mustafa. 1996. "Al-thaqafa wa al-thaqafa al-waqi'iya bayn al-
nadhariya wa al-mumarasa" (Culture and realistic culture between
theory and practice). *Al-Tariq*, January–February.

Dowd, Siobhan. 1993. "Silenced Voices." *Literary Review*, July.

Eagleton, Terry. 2000. *The Idea of Culture*. Oxford: Blackwell.

Fadil, Fadil al-. 2005. "Bairaqdar: Ya ilahi! Hal yakfi an aqul innahu halif li
al-mawt?" (Bairaqdar: Oh God! Is it enough to say that it is death's ally?).
E-mail communication.

Farah, Caesar. 1977. "Censorship and Freedom of Expression in Ottoman
Syria and Egypt." in *Nationalism in a Non-National State: The Dissolu-
tion of the Ottoman Empire*, edited by William W. Haddad and William
Ochsenwald. Columbus: Ohio State University Press.

Fattuh, 'Isa al-. 1994. "Al-salunat al-nisa'iya al-adabiya fi al-'asr al-hadith"
(Women's literary salons in the modern age). *Banat al-ajyal*, no. 9 (January).

Feldman, Noah. 2004. *What We Owe Iraq: War and the Ethics of Nation
Building*. Princeton, N.J.: Princeton University Press.

Fischel, Walter J. 1952. *Ibn Khaldun and Tamerlane*. Berkeley: University
of California Press.

Fontaine, Jean. 1992. "Prose syrienne contemporaine." *IBLA*, no. 169.

Foucault, Michel. 1991 [1977]. *Discipline and Punish: The Birth of the Prison*.
New York: Vintage.

Franklin, H. Bruce, ed. 1998. *Prison Writing in 20th Century America*. New
York: Penguin.

Frazer, J. G. 1976 [1922]. *The Golden Bough: A Study in Magic and Religion*.
London: Macmillan.

Gaston, Cothurne. 1978. "L'essentiel n'est plus de changer le roi." *Peuples
Méditerraneens*, 2.

George, Alan. 2003. *Syria: Neither Bread nor Freedom*. London: Zed Press.

Ghazzi, Nadia al-. 1993. *Shirwal Barhum: Ayyam min Safarbarlik* (Barhum's
baggy pants: Days of the Safarbarlik). Damascus: al-Shadi lil-Nashr wa
al-Tawzi'.

———. 1989. *Hunna: Milaffat wa qadaya* (Women: Files and cases). Damascus: Dar Tlas.

Glain, Stephen. 2005. "Syria at a Crossroads." *Smithsonian Magazine*, July.

Guneratne, Anthony R., and Wimal Dissanayake, eds. 2003. *Rethinking Third Cinema*. New York: Routledge.

Hafiz, Muhammad Walid al-. 1989. *Al-midfa'al-khamis* (The fifth cannon). Damascus: Manshurat Ittihad al-Kuttab al-'Arab.

———. 1985. *Al-khandaq* (The trench). Damascus: Manshurat Ittihad al-Kuttab al-'Arab.

Harlow, Barbara. 1992. *Barred: Women, Writing, and Political Detention*. Hanover, N.H.: Wesleyan University Press.

Havel, Vaclav. 1987. *Living in Truth*. Edited by Jan Vladislav. London: Faber and Faber.

Heath, Stephen. 1976. "Narrative Space." *Screen*, autumn.

Heydemann, Steven. 1999. *Authoritarianism in Syria: Institutions and Social Conflict 1946–1970*. Ithaca, N.Y.: Cornell University Press.

Horowitz, David. 2006. *The Professors: The 101 Most Dangerous Academics in America*. Lanham, Md.: Regnery Publishing.

Human Rights Watch (HRW). 1991. *Syria Unmasked: The Suppression of Human Rights by the Asad Regime*. New York: Human Rights Watch.

Human Rights Watch/Middle East (HRW/ME). 1996. "Syria's Tadmor Prison: Dissent Still Hostage to a Legacy of Terror." *HRW Index*, vol. 8, no. 2E (April). Online.

———. 1995. "Syria: The Price of Dissent." *HRW Index*, vol. 7, no. 4 (July). Online.

Ibn Khaldun. 1969. *The Muqaddimah: An Introduction to History*. Translated by Franz Rosenthal; abridged by N. J. Dawood. Princeton: Princeton University Press.

'Id, 'Abd al-Razzaq. 1993. "Al-riwaya al-suriya: Harb tishrin" (The Syrian novel: The October war). *Qadaya wa Shahadat*, no. 6. Nicosia.

Idilbi, Ulfat. 1991. *Hikayat jaddi* (The story of my grandfather). Damascus: Tlasdar.

———. 1990. *Nafahat Dimashqiya* (Damascene breezes). Damascus: Dar al-Jumhuriya li al-Tibaa.

———. 1980. *Dimashq ya basmat al-huzn* (Damascus, smile of sadness). Translated by P. Clark as *Sabriya*. London: Quartet, 1996.

Ilyas, Mary. 1996. "Li awwal marra ash'uru bil-kitaba ka-hurriya. Li awwal marra ash'uru anna al-kitaba mut'a" (For the first time I feel writing is freedom. For the first time I feel that writing is a pleasure). *Al-Tariq*, 1.1 (January–February): 96–104.

Index on Censorship. 1978–1997. New York: Routledge.

Jaba'i, Ghassan al-. 1995. *Thalath masrahiyat* (Three plays). Damascus: Manshurat Wizarat al-Thaqafa.

———. 1994. *Asabi 'al-mawz* (Banana fingers). Damascus: Manshurat Wizarat al-Thaqafa.

Johnson, Phyllis Berman. 1995. "Blackmail." *Forbes*, 31 July.

Jundi, Tihama al-. 2005. "Al-sha'ir Faraj Bairaqdar: Kana la budda min al-shi'r kay a'rifa nafsi" (Poet Faraj Bairaqdar: Poetry was essential for me to know myself). *Nizwa*, no. 31.

Kaadi, Jurj. 1992. "Muhammad Malas." *Al-Nahar*, 28 December.

Kahf, Mohja. 2001. "The Silences of Contemporary Syrian Literature." *World Literature Today*, spring.

Kassan, Jean al-. 1992. "Shakhsiyat al-'am" (This year's personalities). *Al-Majalla*, 20 December.

Kavanagh, James H. 1990. "Ideology." In *Critical Terms in Literary Study*, edited by Frank Lentricchia and Thomas McLaughlin. Chicago: University of Chicago Press.

Kennedy-Day, Kiki. 2001. "Cinema in Lebanon, Syria, Iraq and Kuwait." In *Companion Encyclopedia of Middle East and North Africa*, edited by Oliver Leaman. New York: Routledge.

Khani, Mallahat al-. 1987. *Imra'a mutalawwina* (A multicolored woman) Damascus: Manshurat Wizarat al-Thaqafa.

———. 1981. *Al-'araba bila jawad* (The horseless carriage). Damascus: Manshurat Ittihad al-Kuttab al-'Arab.

Khuri, Colette al-. 1993. [1979]. *Ayyam ma'a al-ayyam* (Days and days). Damascus: Dar al-Farisa.

———. 1992 [1961]. *Layla wahida* (One night). Damascus: Dar al-Farisa.

———. 1984. *Al-ayyam al-madi'a* (Luminous days). Damascus: Tlasdar.

Khust, Nadia. 1995. *Hubb fi bilad al-Sham* (Love in Syria). Damascus: Ittihad al-Kuttab al-'Arab.

———. 1993. *Dimashq dhakirat al-insan wa al-hajar* (Damascus, memory of people and stones). Damascus: Dar Dania.

———. 1990. *La makan lil-gharib* (No room for the stranger). Damascus: al-Ahali.

———. 1989. *Al-hijra min al-janna* (Departure from Paradise). Damascus: al-Ahali.

———. 1967. *Uhibbu al-Sham* (I love Damascus). N.p.

Kienle, Eberhard, ed. 1994. *Contemporary Syria: Liberalization between Cold War and Cold Peace.* London: I. B. Tauris.

Koelbl, Susanne. 2005. "Das Einmaleins der Diktatur." *Der Spiegel*, 21 February.

Koonz, Claudia. 2003. *The Nazi Conscience.* Cambridge, Mass.: Harvard University Press.

Lobmeyer, Hans Guenther. 1994. *"Al-dimuqratiyya hiyya al-hall?* The Syrian Opposition at the End of the Asad Era." In *Contemporary Syria: Liberalization between Cold War and Cold Peace,* edited by Eberhard Kienle. London: I. B. Tauris.

MacFarquhar, Neil. 2002. "A Nation Challenged: Damascus." *New York Times*, 13 January.

————. 2000. "Hafez al-Assad, Who Turned Syria into a Power in the Middle East, Dies at 69." *New York Times*, 11 June.

Maghut, Muhammad. 2001 [1987]. *Sa akhunu watani* (I shall betray my homeland). Damascus: Dar al-Mada.

Malas, Muhammad. 1991. *Al-manam: Mufakkirat film* (The dream: A film notebook). Beirut: Dar al-Adab.

Masri, Marwan al-, and Muhammad 'Ali Wa'lani. 1988. *Al-katibat al-suriyat 1892–1987* (Syrian women writers 1892–1987). Damascus: al-Ahali.

Midfa'i, Walid. 1996. "Mallahat al-Khani min khilal aqsis thalath majmu'at" (Mallahat al-Khani through stories in three collections). *Al-Baath*, 22 April.

Mina, Hanna. 1997 [1973]. *Sun on a Cloudy Day.* Translated by Barssam Frangich and Clementina Brown. Pueblo, Colo.: Passeggiata Press.

Morris, Norval, and David J. Rothman, eds. 1998. *Oxford History of Prison: The Practice of Punishment in western Society.* Oxford: Oxford University Press.

Munif, 'Abd al-Rahman. 1996. "Ibn Khaldun wa suratuhu fi Munamnamat Ta'rikhiya" (Ibn Khaldun and his image in *Historical Miniatures*). *Al-Tariq*, 1.1: 117–132.

————. 1993. "Al-Thaqafa al-wataniya: Waqi'wa tahaddiyat" (National culture: Reality and challenges). *Qadaya wa Shahedat*, no. 6 (winter).

Naamani, Houda. 1991. *Houda . . . ana al-haqq* (Houda . . . I am thy Lord). Beirut: Dar al-Nahar.

————. 1978. *Adhkuru kuntu nuqta kuntu daira* (I remember I was a point I was a circle). Beirut: Dar al-Nahar.

Neier, Aryeh. 2004. "Bush and Freedom: With Friends Like This." *International Herald Tribune*, 25 January.

Palumbo-Liu, David. 2006. "Preemption, Perpetual War and the Future of the Imagination." *Boundary 2*, 33.1 (spring).

Perthes, Volker. 1994. "Stages of Economic and Political Liberalization." In *Contemporary Syria: Liberalization between Cold War and Cold Peace*, edited by Eberhard Kienle. London. I.B. Tauris.

Peterson, Scott. 1977. "Syrian Soaps Grab Arabs' Prime Time." *Christian Science Monitor*, 2 October, 19.

Porteous, Rebecca, ed. 1995. "*The Dream*: Extracts from a Film Diary by Muhammad Malas." *Alif*, no. 15.

Rahbi, Mayya al-. 1995. *Imra'a mutaharrira li al-'ard* (A liberated woman for sale).

"Repression in Iraq and Syria." 1984. *Index on Censorship*, February.

Robertson, William C. 1990. *Free French Censorship in Syria*. Edinburgh: Edinburgh University Press.

Rosen, Michael, and David Widgery, eds. 1996 [1991]. *The Vintage Book of Dissent*. London: Vintage.

Rushdie, Salman. 2005. "The PEN and the Sword."*New York Times Book Review*,17 April.

Sadiq, Adib [pseud.]. 1990. "The Road to Damascus Is Plagued with Censors." *Index on Censorship*, February.

Said, Edward. 2001. *Power, Politics and Culture: Interviews*. Edited by Gauri Viswanathan. New York: Vintage.

Salamandra, Christa. 2004. *A New Old Damascus: Authenticity and Distinction in Urban Syria*. Bloomington: Indiana University Press.

Samir, Wisal. 1992. *Zaina*. Damascus: al-Ahali.

Samman, Ghada. 1976. *Kawabis Bairut* (Beirut nightmares). Beirut: Dar Ghada al-Samman.

Samu'il, Ibrahim. 1994. *Al-wa'r al-azraq* (The blue wasteland). Damascus: Dar al-Jundi.

———. 1990. *Al-nahnahat* (Light coughs). Damascus: Dar al-Jundi.

———. 1988. *Ra'ihat al-khatw al-thaqil* (The stench of heavy steps). Damascus: Dar al-Jundi.

Sardar, Ziauddin. 2004. *Desperately Seeking Paradise: Journeys of a Sceptical Muslim*. London: Grantan.

Seale, Patrick. 1989. *Asad: The Struggle for the Middle East*. Berkeley: University of California Press.

Seurat, Marie. 1988. *Corbeaux d'Alep* (The ravens of Aleppo). Paris: Gallimard.

Shafik, Viola. 1998. *Arab Cinema: History and Cultural Identity*. Cairo: American University of Cairo Press.

Shakir, Iman Husayn. 1996. "Ma wara' al-ihtilal absha' minhu" (What is behind the occupation is uglier). *Al-Safir al-Thaqafi*, 5 January.

Sharif, Mahir al-. 1995. "Sa'dallah Wannus wa *Munamnamat Tarikhiya*" (Sa'dallah Wannus and *Historical Miniatures*). *Al-Nahj*, summer.

Shohat, Ella, and Robert Stam. 1994. *Unthinking Eurocentrism: Multiculturalism and the Media*. New York: Routledge.

Slyomovics, Susan. 2005. *The Performance of Human Rights in Morocco*. Philadelphia: University of Pennsylvania Press.

——. 1998. *The Object of Memory*. Philadelphia: University of Pennsylvania Press.

Talbi, Mohamed. 1973. *Ibn Haldun et l'Histoire*. Tunis: Maison Tunisienne de l'Edition.

Tawq, Louisa. 1993. "20 Years of Searching for Himself with the Camera." *Al-Usbu' al-'Arabi*, 4 January.

Taylor, Stuart, Jr. 2006. "The Man Who Would Be King." *Atlantic Monthly*, April.

"Testimony of an Ex-Censor." 1987. *Index on Censorship*, June.

'Ujayli, 'Abd al-Salam al-. 1987. *Maut al-habiba* (Death of the beloved). Damascus: Tlasdar.

Valls, Jorge. 1986. *20 Years and 40 Days: A Life in a Cuban Prison*. New York: Americas Watch.

Van Dam, Nikolaos. 1996. *The Struggle for Power in Syria: Politics and Society under Asad and the Ba'th Party*. New York: I. B. Tauris.

Verdery, Katherine. 1991. *National Ideology under Socialism: Identity and Cultural Politics in Ceausescu's Romania*. Berkeley: University of California Press.

Wannus, Sa'adallah. 1996. *Al-a'mal al-kamila* (Complete works in 3 volumes). 3 vols. Damascus: Al-Ahali.

Wedeen, Lisa. 1999. *Ambiguities of Domination: Politics, Rhetoric, and Symbols in Contemporary Syria*. Chicago: University of Chicago Press.

Williams, Raymond. 1983 [1958]. *Culture and Society 1780–1950*. New York: Columbia University Press.

Zayyat, Latifa al-. 2004. "Testimonial of a Creative Woman." *Adab wa naqd*, no. 135 (November 1996). Translated by 'Ali Badran and Margot Badran in *Opening the Gates: Arab Feminist Writings*, edited by Margot Badran and miriam cooke. Bloomington: Indiana University Press.

Žižek, Slavoj. 2004. *Iraq: The Borrowed Kettle*. New York: Verso.

——. 2001. *Did Somebody Say Totalitarianism? Five Interventions in the (Mis)use of a Notion*. New York: Verso.

———. 2000. "Da Capo Sensa Fine." In *Contingency, Hegemony, Universality: Contemporary Dialogues on the Left*, edited by J. Butler, E. Laclau, and S. Žižek. New York: Verso.

———, ed. 1994. *Mapping Ideology*. New York: Verso.

miriam cooke is a professor of Arab culture at Duke University. She is the author of *Women Claim Islam: Creating Islamic Feminism through Literature* (2001); *Hayati, My Life: A Novel* (2000); *Women and the War Story* (1998); and *War's Other Voices: Women Writers on the Lebanese Civil War* (1987, 1996). She has also edited (with Bruce Lawrence) *Muslim Networks from Hajj to Hip Hop* (2005); (with Margot Badran) *Opening the Gates: A Century of Arab Feminist Writing* (2nd ed., 2004); (with Roshni Rustomji-Kerns) *Blood into Ink: South Asian and Middle Eastern Women Write War* (1994); and (with Angela Woollacott) *Gendering War Talk* (1993).

CIP data TO COME